THE BUSINESS GUIDE TO EFFECTIVE WRITING

THE BUSINESS GUIDE TO EFFECTIVE WRITING

Revised second edition

J A Fletcher &
D F Gowing

Kogan Page

First published in 1979 by the Institute of Chartered Accountants in England and Wales entitled *Effective Writing for Accountants.*

Second, revised edition published in 1987 by Kogan Page Limited entitled *The Business Guide to Effective Writing*. Reprinted 1989, 1991.

Kogan Page Limited
120 Pentonville Road
London N1 9JN

British Library Cataloguing in Publication Data

A CIP record for this book is available from the British Library.

ISBN 1-85091-291-2 (paperback)
ISBN 1-85091-428-1 (hardback)

Printed and bound in Great Britain by
Biddles Limited, Guildford

Contents

Preface

The paperless office is as far away as ever. A nation of shopkeepers has become a nation of writers. At the same time most people who work at desks are surprised how difficult it is to write a letter, how long it takes, and how badly other people do it.

Grammar and acceptable style change slowly; technology moves fast. Both influence writers, and this book attempts to help them deal with both.

We cover the essential grammar for those who have forgotten what they ever knew. We try to help those who have plenty to write, but get stuck in selecting and sorting first. We concentrate on making writing not just correct but efficient, because reports and letters have to earn their keep. Recent technology can help to produce a first class document at a relatively low cost.

Although this book is written first for adults, it will be useful also for students of business studies. Most other books in this field assume that readers know what parts of speech are, and can spot an active or a passive verb without help. Our experience of running courses for professional institutions, firms and public authorities is that many writers in mid-career are lost at this point; and students should also find it helpful. Essential grammar (there isn't much, but what is essential is not easy) we explain with examples.

Business and professional people build up experience in collecting and analysing information in the early stages of their careers, and draw on their previous education to help them present this information to others. Later the emphasis shifts. They find they are spending a rising proportion of their time on presentation, especially written presentation, and that their general education may not have prepared them adequately for this.

Professional bodies recognise the value of 'continuing professional education' in which members are encouraged to extend their range of competence and refurbish their basic skills. While courses may be the best way to provide much of this, either externally or in-house, it is valuable to learn independently, whether through audio cassettes, interactive video or publications.

The book is divided into two parts. In Part 1 we deal first, in Chapter 1, with what the writers are trying to achieve; and second in the remaining chapters of Part 1 with how they should actually write to achieve it. Then Part 2 looks at specific kinds of writing in which business and professional people engage.

J A Fletcher
D F Gowing

January 1987

Acknowledgements

We are grateful for permission to reproduce as follows:

Figure 1, p.91, from the IATA Annual Report, 1986, with the kind permission of IATA Management Information Division;

Figure 2, p.92, with the kind permission of the British Institute of Management, from their 1985 Annual Report;

Figure 3, p.93, with the kind permission of the Royal Borough of Windsor and Maidenhead, from the 1986 publication 'The Way Ahead';

Figure 4, p.93, with the kind permission of the Anglia Building Society, from their 1985 Annual Report and Accounts;

Appendices 1 and 2.1, pp.99 and 100, from the 'Report of the Company Law Committee' (June 1962, Cmnd 1749) with the kind permission of the Controller of Her Majesty's Stationery Office;

Appendix 2.2, p.101, from 'Hours into Minutes', by Dr P J C Perry, OBE, obtainable from the British Association for Commercial and Industrial Education, 16 Park Crescent, London W1N 4AP;

Appendix 2.3, p.102, from a guide to 'Format Standards for Scientific and Technical Reports' (December 1973, DRIC Specification 1000), with the kind permission of Her Majesty's Stationery Office and the Ministry of Defence;

In Appendix 8, p.123, the poem 'I heard the happy lark exult' by A P Herbert, from 'What a Word!', with the kind permission of A P Watt Limited.

Part 1. Principles

Chapter 1

What Shall I Put In?

Use

In judging the effectiveness of an implement, such as a kitchen knife, a garden fork, or a surgical instrument, we consider its intended use. Similarly, if we were designing these implements we would attempt to satisfy the user's needs, and we would expect to be judged by how far we had met those needs. If we were asked to design a map, we would choose a small scale for route planning, and a large scale to show the individual buildings, car parks and footpaths. We are accustomed to planning and judging everyday things in the light of their intended use, not as works of art.

But writing is seldom considered in the way that we plan and judge everything else. It is usually considered in a vacuum, where the only significant criterion of good writing is good style and grammar. Probably the reason for this is the way English was traditionally taught at school, particularly by writing essays. This is not incorrect, as good style and grammar are important attributes of effective writing, but they do not in themselves make a piece of writing effective. Not many adults write essays as part of their work.

Like anything else, to be effective, a document must satisfy the user's needs. This means writers must know two things:

- what needs they are attempting to satisfy
- who the users are (readers).

In addition, writers should know before they begin

- technical content: the information necessary to put in the document;
- scope: whether there are any special items that they must include;
- limits: whether any items are specifically excluded;
- deadline: how long they have to write the document;
- house rules: a working knowledge of the rules and practice of their own organisation.

Having accepted that writing is judged by reference to its 'use', the writer must define 'use' correctly. The 'use' is not in reading or understanding the document; it is in enabling the reader to decide what to do.

Most writers tend to define their purpose first of all in terms of telling; they are writing to tell someone something. Usually it is possible and better to describe the purpose as what the reader is to do. In other words the effectiveness of a report or letter is not measured simply by the information it imparts but by the action that results from it.

Thus in the appraisal of a new project it is not enough to give relevant particulars such as projected income, costs, pay-back period and the rest; the report should present alternative courses of action clearly differentiated, and highlight criteria for the success of the new project, so that those who have to take the decision are properly able to do so.

The writer must know the use or purpose of a document to write it effectively because this use will determine

- what is relevant
- presentation, sequence, and headings
- arguments or methods of persuasion
- language, words and sentences.

For example, in the post-audit management letter, sometimes called a letter of weakness, part of the use is to enable the client to correct malpractices and omissions. To write such a letter effectively, the auditor–writer must think what presentation, arguments and phraseology will be most likely to achieve this result. So in every working document, unless the writer knows what the readers are to do after reading the document, it is unlikely that they will do it.

Relevance

Most writers are aware of the problem of relevance: what to put in and what to leave out. Those who have little clear idea of the reader's purpose will have little clear idea of what information will be relevant. Relevance is a relationship. What is relevant to a particular piece of writing is that which is relevant to its purpose, namely to enable the reader to do something, such as make a decision.

A document can be thoroughly relevant to the subject without being relevant to the use or the reader, and it is then an irrelevant document. For instance, if the purpose were to analyse and improve a financial control system, how that system arose may be relevant to the system (the subject) but not necessarily to the use of the document. Again, if the purpose of an investigation report were to help decide whether to lend to a firm, the date of the firm's establishment might be irrelevant; but for an issuing house, preparing to meet the requirements of the law and the Stock Exchange in a prospectus, such information would be essential.

The document must be relevant to the readers as well as the purpose or use. This particularly applies to the definitions and explanations of the growing number of technical terms that business people and the professions use. The term 'historic cost' will require explanation to a layman, but such explanation would be irrelevant, and even insulting, to an accountant. When the phrase 'prepared under the historic cost convention' was first used, laymen assumed there was something different about the accounts described in this new way, which was precisely the opposite of what the statement was supposed to imply.

Defining the purpose: terms of reference

Certain purposes can be taken as applying to any document, and therefore need not be stated each time:

- to be a good advertisement for the source;
- to improve relations with the client or the public;
- to avoid or prevent legal action.

For instance, auditors commonly have to make recommendations to protect themselves and their firms from an action for negligence, even if they suspect that these recommendations will be ignored.

Where the writer of a report is also the originator, the purpose ought to be clear. Even then it is important to write it down, so that it is equally clear to any others involved in producing it at the time, and reading it, possibly years later.

Where the originator is different from the writer, the originator is responsible for stating the purpose. It is like any other delegation; both duty and interest require the originator to discuss it fully with the writer. If they cannot work out together written 'terms of reference', which are the purpose of the report, then the writer should draft a statement of purpose and submit this to the originator.

If the report or document is one of a series, as with a monthly management report, the first report of the series should give the purpose of the series. The terms of reference need not be spelt out on each later report. However, if the purpose is not stated in writing at all, or if it is stated once and then forgotten, there is a danger that the document will appear in the same form time after time, when the original purpose has changed. New staff simply copy last month's, or last year's, report, 'because we've always done it that way', not because it is effective. Reports written regularly need to be queried regularly, to confirm that the original purposes are still applicable and that the document still meets the purposes.

Written terms of reference may go further than stating the purpose, and include much of the information which the originator must give the writer if the writer is to write a good relevant report. What the writer needs is listed on p.13. The originator cannot give the technical information; that is for the writer to find out. He need not give the appropriate house rules. But the terms of reference should include:

- the purpose or use of the document;
- the intended readership and confidentiality;
- the scope and limits of the content;
- the deadline or time-scale for writing the document;
- any other resources and money needed and authorised for preparing the document;
- the authority needed to collect evidence.

While the writer may not need all of this in a given instance, it is well to check that as much of this as possible is available. It is worth reading the terms of reference of previous reports (see Appendix 1 for an example).

The terms of reference are not a permanent restriction. They can be changed by agreement as the investigation proceeds, if necessary. Sometimes Royal Commissions go outside their terms of reference deliberately. Then they make it clear that they have done so, and why.

Official terms of reference are mainly suitable for official, or long, documents, but the ideas apply to any writing. Even short documents are better for a suitably brief statement of purpose, as when a memorandum begins 'I am writing to confirm . . .' A writer who has no clear idea what a document is for, cannot know what is relevant, and the seniors who authorise it cannot expect the document to be much use.

The writer who does receive written terms of reference should check that they are stated in a way that makes them usable for sifting the evidence. If the reader is X, the subject of the report Y, and the purpose Z, the terms of reference should follow the formula:

to enable X to use Y to achieve Z

and not just:

to inform X about Y.

Thus it is not enough for the terms of reference for a monthly report from the management accountant to the sales director to say: 'to inform the sales director of monthly sales by individual sales representatives'. This may be a true statement of what it is expected to contain, but it stops short of giving the purpose. A more useful way of expressing the terms of reference would be: 'to enable the sales director to evaluate the performance and targets of individual sales personnel, and to take any action necessary, in the light of reported monthly variances in sales'. This would more obviously help the writer to produce a useful document, perhaps including some factors which by the previous formula would have been irrelevant.

The readers

The characteristics of your readers will influence what is the most effective way of writing to them. Ideally you need to know about:

- *their language.* Whether they speak and read British English, American English, or some other language; what technical and professional language they talk.
- *their education.* What assumptions you can make and what explanations you must give.
- *their knowledge.* Particularly how much they already know about the subject discussed in the document.
- *their priorities.* What do they believe important?
- *their customs.* What are their prejudices? What will they agree to readily, and where will they need a lot of convincing?
- *their motives.* Are they primarily concerned with profits, or turnover, or personal prestige, or power, or size of unit, or number of staff under their control, or expense accounts, or quality of product, or the environment, or service to the community? With professional people, such as doctors,

lawyers, teachers, scientists, and accountants, are they concerned first with loyalty to other members of the profession?

- *their authority.* How free to act are they? Can they decide on your recommendations by themselves? If not, to whom do they go? What arguments will they need to persuade those who have the necessary authority?

Finding this information about the readers is difficult. The writer will never know everything about the reader that would be useful, but this is a poor argument for not trying to find out as much as possible. Writers should:

- *Meet the reader.* It is always easier to write to someone you have met. The way people talk, the books and papers in their room, the judgements they make about other matters, will suggest answers to many of the questions about readers.
- *If you cannot meet, try the telephone.* Some of the characteristics that would be apparent at a meeting may be evident from a telephone conversation. On the other hand, those who are not used to telephoning, or dislike it, may have a 'telephone personality' which differs from their real one.
- *Read what your reader has written.* Look up correspondence. Both the content and style of letters may provide clues about the best way to write back. If you cannot find letters, reports may help; but they are more likely to have been revised by colleagues or seniors.
- *Consider the reader's job.* If you cannot meet, or talk by telephone, or read their writing, make the most of the information you nearly always have, or can guess: the job. To some extent the choice of job is affected by personality. Some jobs require specialised training, perhaps after years of education; they are a guide to loyalties and priorities; they determine the frame of reference or 'window' through which people see the world; they require a certain language and special analytical tools with which those in that particular job solve the problems appropriate to it.

  We all like to imagine that our particular expertise will be needed to solve any given problem; which is why what is a mechanical engineering problem to a mechanical engineer, will seem to an accountant to be basically financial, while a personnel officer may well redefine it as a matter of staff relations. When you write to someone in another profession or job, you should allow for this. Remember that this approach should be something of a last resort. It can lead to generalisation, and should not override information available about particular individuals.

Chapter 2

Structure

What structure is

The structure of anything is the way it is built or put together; its arrangement. In biology it refers to the component parts of an organism. In a man-made thing, it is the plan or outline of the thing, or perhaps of its principal parts. It might be the organisation chart of an organisation, or the programme of events in an entertainment.

Structure is the main difference between a casual conversation and an interview, between a friendly social letter and a business one, or between an accidental meeting and a committee. In the structured event there is an aim, and the structure is the plan to meet that aim. Most of the unsatisfactory communications we receive at work are the result of having an aim, but not being structured properly.

In writing letters, memoranda, and reports, the structure consists basically of the initial plan. There are several points to be made; what are they? in what order should they be made? what are the sections into which this communication naturally falls? When these questions are answered, we have a list of points in order, which will often serve as the headings and sub-headings of the document. If the points need to be numbered, this is also a matter of structure.

If the headings and numbering of the document are satisfactory, the battle for an effective communication is half won. The other half is the actual words and sentences of the text under the headings, which we call 'style'. As it is style that is the main focus of attention in school English, it is often forgotten that structure is the critical part of a working document.

Particular structures

Written documents include forms, memoranda, letters, notes

and reports. These terms are neither precisely defined nor mutually exclusive, but the differences between them are largely differences of structure and headings. A form has a fixed set of headings, which the form designer makes, and the form-filler has a restricted box in which to add the appropriate text for the heading. It is in a sense the most efficient structure; the form-filler does not have to worry about choosing headings, the amount of space for writing under each is specified, and the reader knows exactly where to find each bit of information.

Some reports resemble forms; for instance school reports, or laboratory reports, where the structure is predictable and repeated. But usually a report is a long document in which the writer has to invent headings, decide the sequence, and decide how much text should go under each heading.

A letter is a ceremonial and courteous document between different organisations, or between individuals not responsible to the same employer, or on special occasions (for instance, a letter confirming recruitment or unusual leave) between people within one organisation. The most obvious characteristic of a letter is the opening salutation 'Dear . . .' and the ending 'Yours sincerely' or some similar phrase. Usually a letter has fewer headings and sub-headings than a report, and less numbering or none at all.

A memorandum is really a letter between two or more people in one organisation, with less elaborate courtesy than a letter; usually the 'Dear' and the 'Yours sincerely' bits are left out of memos. But it may well have headings and numbering, and a long memorandum is a report in almost every way. The post-audit management letter is a letter with many of the characteristics of a report, and some firms do in fact divide this letter into a report and a covering letter.

The way 'report', 'memorandum', 'letter', and 'notes' are used is conventional, and the nearest thing to a distinguishing characteristic is the duration of their expected importance. Letters may be important for months, notes and memos for days or weeks, reports commonly for many years.

Planning the structure

It is best to plan the structure of an important report twice: once when the terms of reference are known but nothing else, when the writer can estimate the reader's expectations unaffected by the result of the investigation; and a second time after the investigation is over. Then the results will be uppermost in the writer's mind, but the first draft of the structure will be a reminder of the reader's expectations. The sequence of events would thus be:

- agree terms of reference
- draft provisional structure; file it
- conduct investigation
- revise draft structure
- write report to revised structure.

It can be difficult to plan the structure if you are submerged by the details and worries of the investigation. On the other hand, planning the structure of the report before collecting the evidence may be a help towards planning the investigation itself.

Headings, good and bad

Headings considered singly, should be:

- *explicit.* The reader must be able to tell from the heading (possibly in the context of other headings) exactly what the words beneath the heading are about. Headings like 'Miscellaneous', 'Facilities', and 'Other factors' fail to say anything.
- *brief.* One word is good; five is acceptable; more than three-quarters of a line is probably too long.

A set of headings should be:

- *comprehensive.* Make sure everything is covered.
- *mutually exclusive.* It is almost as annoying to find that the point you are interested in is under two headings as under none.
- *in a logical sequence.* This does not always mean in order of importance; look at some possible rearrangements. There is unlikely to be only one logical arrangement. Make sure that the logic of the sequence is the reader's.

Numbering

Purpose

Numbering, like other aspects of the working document, is not done for fun; it does help to give an air of efficiency and professionalism to the document, but the real purpose is to aid in reference afterwards, at meetings or in other documents, and the kind of numbering largely depends on this.

There are many numbering systems from which the writer can choose. The most basic ones are:

- continuous paragraph numbering, which we call the Civil Service system;
- the traditional alpha-numeric system;
- the decimal (1.1.1) system.

Others are usually compromises between these, or a mixture of them.

Headings and paragraphs

The Civil Service system is to number paragraphs consecutively from 1 onwards to the end of the document. It looks neat, and it makes precise reference to any paragraph easy, even with a complicated report.

The main disadvantage is in preparation; the numbering of each paragraph cannot be settled until the final paragraph has been written. If another paragraph is added after the numbers have been allocated, all the subsequent numbers would have to change, and all the cross-references in the report would be affected. Word processors can do this tedious job quickly, so this particular drawback has less force than it used to have.

Another disadvantage is that it is difficult to refer to a section simply by paragraph numbers. It is more complicated to say 'Powers of Taxation and Fiscal Arrangements, paragraphs 186 to 203' than to say 'Chapter 9' or 'Section 9.4'. So in practice many Civil Service documents also number the chapters or sections.

The traditional numbering system numbers headings rather than paragraphs, and uses letters as well as numbers. Thus the headings might be 1, 2, 3, and the sub-headings lettered a, b, c, or (a), (b), (c). Sub-sub-headings would be another kind of number, usually roman numerals using lower case letters: (i), (ii), (iii). For a fourth tier of numbering, capital letters (A, B, C) are available, and generally used for the chief headings. In this way letters and numbers can identify alternate levels of heading and sub-heading, which helps: C 3 (a) (iv) is clearer than C (c) 1 (iv), particularly when spoken. The drawback to the system involving letters is that there are only 26 letters in the alphabet, and (i) might be either the ninth letter of the alphabet or the roman numeral for 1. But the system is widely known and used, and works well for simple documents.

The system most frequently used, however, is neither of these, but what is called the decimal system: 1.1 is the number of the first sub-heading of the first heading. The great merit of this system, in which headings are numbered rather than paragraphs, or as well as paragraphs, is that numbers do not run out (whereas letters do); and the number shows exactly the relation between each heading and each sub-heading.

It is also true that the writer can place layer upon layer, but this temptation to have 4.5.3.8.6 is considered by many its gravest drawback. Certainly several layers of heading and sub-heading are a sign of clumsy writing in any system; and in this one it is apt to lead to spots before the eyes. Three layers of heading should be enough for all normal documents; more are undesirable except in manuals of instruction.

The decimal numbering system is increasingly accepted by business and the professions; it is used by British Standards and similar European standards; and educated readers will understand it without difficulty.

The chief disadvantage is that if it is used to number headings but not paragraphs, reference to a small part of a report is difficult where there is a long gap between headings. In such cases the 'mesh' of the reference may not be fine enough to cater for all those who need to refer to the report later. But the best answer to that is to have frequent headings.

For most purposes the decimal system will be best. It is flexible enough to cover a wide range of documents, and is therefore ideal for a house style. There are many other systems available, and more may be invented; some are a mixture of the three described, and they will have a mixture of the advantages and disadvantages accordingly. The main thing is to have some suitable system rather than none.

Lists, appendices and pages

It is often necessary to have a list of items within a paragraph, or even within a sentence:

> *'The choice between buying and leasing premises depends on the company's*
> *a. capital resources*
> *b. expected rate of return on capital*
> *c. experience of maintaining its own premises.'*

Clearly here the numbering of each item in the list is not part of the numbering system for headings and paragraphs; and if possible the numbers or letters used for the list should be as distinct from the others as the system permits. Probably the best combination is to use the decimal system with only arabic numerals for headings, sub-headings, or paragraphs, and lower case letters for lists within a sentence. See Appendix 2.1 for an example.

Appendices should be numbered as 'Appendix 1', 'Appendix 2' and so on; or 'Appendix A' or 'Appendix I'. Arabic numerals are more common, but capital letters distinguish an appendix more clearly from a decimally numbered text. One appendix should be 'The Appendix', not 'Appendix 1', as the use of a number implies that there is more than one.

If an appendix is long, the sections, paragraphs, or headings may be numbered. They should form a self-contained system. Therefore, when referring to a passage within an appendix, the appendix number must also be quoted.

Number the pages in continuous sequence from page 1 to the last page of the last appendix. Some books have a different numbering for the pages up to the table of contents (usually roman numerals in lower case letters, (i), (ii), (iii), etc.) and the normal arabic numerals from the first page of the text following. There seems no reason for doing this within working documents, and it introduces an element of ambiguity if page 1 could be two different pages. Ideally, keep the same numbering sequence for all pages from the title-page to the last page of the last appendix.

If an appendix to a report is another report (not unusual), some conflict between the numbering systems of the documents may arise. It may be useful to have two page numbers on each page; one devised for the appendix-report originally, possibly used for cross-reference within itself, and the other for the embracing report. The numbers are usually so different that confusion does not arise. The place on the page (such as top right or bottom centre) may also help to identify which series each belongs to.

There are examples of the main kinds of numbering in Appendix 2.

Chapter 3

Style and Grammar

Grammar

Incorrect grammar or usage is undignified, looks uneducated, undermines the reader's confidence in the writer's efficiency and professionalism, leads to ambiguity, and wastes time while the reader looks at the incorrect passage again. This is why it is necessary to polish the draft of an important document.

Unfortunately, correct grammar, and grammar acceptable to the various readers, are not the same. Acceptable grammar is not necessarily correct, as some readers are not grammatically critical; and what is grammatically correct is not necessarily acceptable to all. Some readers have superstitions of their own about what is 'good grammar', based often on what they learnt at school from an impressive but not well informed teacher.

With spelling an agreed dictionary can settle disputes. But few take a similarly disputed point of grammar to an acknowledged authority such as Fowler's *Modern English Usage*. Perhaps the *Oxford Paperback Dictionary*, which includes comments on usage, is doing good service here by extending the authority of the Dictionary to matters of grammar and usage; though a separate book is necessary for the professional writer. And for every person who consults a standard work on English style and usage there are a hundred who are so convinced of their own expertise that they see no need to look it up.

Among the reasons why people who may be happy to use a dictionary do not refer to authorities on style are:

- that grammar is believed to be personal, subjective, and arbitrary, and that no two books or authorities agree anyway. This proposition is about as untrue as it would be of spelling. The differences are insignificant compared with the agreement.
- that as the language is developing, a grammar may be out of date. However, an up-to-date guide to English usage is as valuable and reliable as an equivalent dictionary.

- that specialists need to use their own words in their own ways for their own purposes; which makes books on the subject by non-specialists valueless. But in practice there are hardly any words or phrases, apart from technical terms where ambiguity is unlikely, which specialists need to use differently from other people. As they are writing to other people, this is just as well.

Principles, authentic and spurious

Authentic principles are those on which the leading authorities agree. They are explained by the arbiters of style accepted widely: Fowler in *The King's English* and *Modern English Usage*, this last revised by Sir Ernest Gowers; and the classic *Complete Plain Words* by Gowers, revised (1986) by Greenbaum and Whitcut.

The sceptic will ask: but who says these people are right? It is true that we have no 'Académie Anglaise' to regulate the language. But, first, these authorities are more widely accepted in educated circles than in any others; and second, they do not advance their principles as arbitrary ones. In each case they give a reason for their advice. So we can say that an authentic principle is not only authoritative, it is also justifiable logically.

By contrast there are many principles that are held by the badly informed and specifically condemned by these books. There are two interesting articles in Fowler's *Modern English Usage*, under 'Fetishes' and 'Superstitions' respectively, that list these misguided beliefs. Such ideas do much to make writing unnecessarily difficult. We call them spurious principles.

The best illustration of a spurious principle is the rule that it is wrong to begin a sentence with 'and' or 'but'. There are few of us who have not been drilled into following this rule at some stage of our education.

Yet virtually every master of the English language uses these words freely to begin sentences. The Authorised version of the English Bible begins more sentences, and indeed chapters, with 'and' than with any other word. Shakespeare often begins sentences, and begins three sonnets, with 'but'. There is a sentence beginning 'and' or 'but' on nearly every page of Dickens; and so with all the great writers. The authorities all condemn this alleged rule as nonsense.

Why did it originate? It is hard to see; yet it is so firmly believed that many will not easily accept the evidence against it.

It is the kind of rule that a writer may do well to keep, simply to avoid offending; but if you can do anything to explode the myths, as we have done in this book by breaking the spurious rules, you will make the job of writing much easier for those who come after.

We believe that specialists ought to know both the authentic rules and the spurious ones; and in Appendix 8 we have included all the authentic principles that specialists frequently break, and the spurious principles that in our experience readers are likely to believe.

To improve your style bear these points in mind:

- know your readers: see pp.17-18. Assess how important it is to them that you keep real or spurious grammatical rules.
- keep by you the recommended works of reference on usage (see Appendix 7).
- set yourself a high standard as a writer, but be tolerant of the failings of other writers.
- remember that the style is good if you put the message across so that the reader does not even think of the grammatical points.
- some people have an instinct for grammar and usage. If you are not such a person, ask someone who is to read your draft and mark any passages that need changing.

The paragraph

A paragraph has two roles:

- logically, it helps the reader follow the argument, by indicating when the document is moving on to make a new point.
- visually, it breaks up the appearance of the page and makes it look interesting and readable.

Logically, if a paragraph is to enable the reader to see separate steps in an argument, each paragraph should be unified. If it is unified it should be possible to devise a heading for it. If the heading is imprecise, such as 'Miscellaneous' or 'Facilities', the paragraph may not be unified; perhaps it should be broken up into two or more paragraphs. If there could be a heading that would describe the subject of the paragraph and so serve as a signpost to the text, then the paragraph is a unified paragraph.

Visually. Too many paragraphs on the page look jerky; too few give the reader no breathing space. The end of a paragraph is the reader's chance to stop and let the ideas sink in. The visually 'right' paragraph length will depend on other visual factors:

- the size of the page
- the typography
- the margins and spaces between blocks of text
- headings
- colour
- tables, lists, illustrations or other breaks in the visual continuity. Newspapers, for instance, rely on all these, and on columns, to make up an attractive page.

To provide a standard for the lengths of paragraphs for different kinds of working document, it is helpful to measure the lengths of paragraphs in different documents that are recognised as readable. Our observations are:

	Average number of	
	Lines	Sentences
	per paragraph	
Quality newspaper	10	1.5
Popular newspaper	6	1
Tax return guide	5	2
A4 typescript report	4	2

The sentence

Most people can write grammatically acceptable sentences. Basically, a sentence must have a verb, which is a doing word like 'come' or 'manage' or 'assess', and a subject, that is, the noun that does the doing word: 'Mr Smith' or 'inflation' or 'we'. The basic part of the sentence is simply this essential part: 'Mr Smith came . . .' or 'We will assess . . .'. The sentences in any book are all made up of one or more such basic sentences linked with each other or with other words in supporting roles, filling out the meaning. All this may seem elementary; but in our experience people do sometimes write a sentence like: 'With reference to your memorandum of 4th March on the above subject' which has neither verb nor subject.

Much of the poor writing that does exist, and many of the faults of grammar, result simply from sentences that are too long. Most people have no idea how long their sentences are; if asked, they guess between 8 and 20 words a sentence. In fact this would be too short for an average sentence, particularly for a trained specialist reader. A good piece of writing may even contain a few sentences of 50 or 60 words, but you have to be a good writer to get away with that. Those who like numerical guidelines may find these helpful:

- It is monotonous to have three consecutive sentences all within 10 per cent of the same length. Vary the length.
- The total number of words in four consecutive sentences should usually be between 80 and 160 words.
- If you are writing to readers less well educated than yourself, write shorter sentences. To the general public, in four consecutive sentences there should not be more than 120 words altogether.
- If the subject matter is complex, or needs slow study and close concentration, break it up into small parts, either by providing a list, or by shorter sentences.

Active and passive

All verbs are either active or passive, and writers of professional documents should be aware of the difference between them, and the advantages of each. Ignorance of this is likely to lead to the habit of writing in the passive, and to this kind of sentence: 'If the confirmation of sales can be credited by the sales office and satisfactory results can be obtained from changes in procedure, the necessity for an interim examination would be obviated.'

The following examples show the difference between active and passive:

Active	*Passive*
Competition affects prices.	Prices are affected by competition.
The auditor checked the invoices.	The invoices were checked by the auditor.
The invoices arrived.	The invoices were delivered.

The difference can be expressed symbolically:

Active	*Passive*
X does Y.	Y is done by X.
X does.	Y is done.
X does Y to Z.	Y is done by X to Z.

The active starts with the agent, the person or thing who does something, then gives the verb, which is what the agent does, and then may say to whom or what the agent did it. The passive starts with the person or thing that is done, then gives the verb, which is what is done or was done, and may end by saying who did it. The doer comes first in the active, whereas in the passive the doer comes last, or is left out altogether.

You can see from the examples:

- an active sentence can always be changed into a passive one, and often a passive can be turned into an active;
- the passive version, if it means the same as the active, is two words longer;
- the first extra word in the passive is the verb, and is part of the verb 'to be': for instance, 'was', 'are', or 'were';
- the word after the part of the verb 'to be' is always in the past participle of the verb in the active version: 'affected', 'checked'. Most participles end '-ed';
- the second extra word in the passive where the meaning is the exact equivalent of the active, is the word 'by'. This serves to join the doer, who came first in the active version, on to the end of the passive version.

Always prefer the active form for the following reasons:

- it is easier to understand. The passive sentences given so far are admittedly not difficult to follow; but in the long sentences that are normal and possibly inevitable in professional writing, the passive form makes understanding more difficult still.
- the passive tends to make for longer sentences, not only because it uses more words for the same meaning, but also because it encourages the use of abstract nouns. For example:
  - The auditor inspected the invoices: active, 5 words.
  - The invoices were inspected by the auditor: passive, 7 words.
  - The inspection of the invoices was carried out by the auditor: passive with the abstract noun 'inspection', 11 words.
- where writers are in the habit of using the passive in the form that omits the doer, such as 'we were advised' or 'it was thought', they will not be saying who gave the advice or whether they agreed with it, and whether it was the writer or someone else who thought it. These may be serious omissions.

Despite the advantages of writing in the active, the passive may be necessary or preferable:

- when the doer is irrelevant: 'Bills totalling £2,345 were accepted in July'.
- where there is a reason for concealing the doer's identity: 'Three letters of credit were mislaid.'
- where the doer is unknown.
- as a way of changing the style to keep the reader's interest.

There are three ways of changing from passive to active:

- change 'Y was done by X' into 'X did Y'. This is the easiest way provided the writer knows who X is.
- change the verb: 'Assets were reduced by . . .' becomes 'Assets fell by . . .'.
- change the subject: 'These recommendations can be implemented by two methods' can become 'There are two methods for implementing these recommendations.'

We can now translate the passives in the sentence given at the beginning of this section into actives, using each of the three methods just given:

Passive	*Active*	*Method*
If the confirmation of sales can be credited by the sales office and	If the sales office can credit the confirmation of sales and changes	(X and Y)
satisfactory results can be obtained from changes in	in procedure bring satisfactory results, the	(changed verb)
procedure, the necessity for an interim examination would be obviated.	interim examination would be unnecessary.	(changed subject)
(31 words)	(23 words)	

The two places where writers are particularly likely to use the passive, and where it is particularly dangerous, are the terms of reference, and the recommendations. It is tempting to say 'We were asked to investigate . . .'; but the authority of the report depends on knowing who asked. Do not be shy about naming names. In the recommendations 'It is recommended that . . . be done', with two passives, is a frequent form. Often the report leaves open or vague exactly who recommended, and who should do whatever was recommended. 'We recommend' may seem too definite and final (though that can be an advantage; see Appendix 2.1) and 'it is recommended' may suggest that the recommendation comes from the client rather than the writer, the reader rather than the writer, which may be supposed to make it more acceptable. But that is not much use if those who accept it assume that someone else will implement it.

It ought to be possible to achieve most of these advantages while still writing in the active. 'We recommend' can become 'we propose', 'we suggest' or 'we consider'; and when the points have been agreed in advance, 'we confirm the following agreed recommendations'.

The word

When children are learning English at school they are often encouraged to use long words, to increase their vocabulary. It may feel unnatural to do the opposite; yet for adults, engaged in writing professionally to those perhaps less well educated than they are, it is a waste of time and causes misunderstanding to use long words unnecessarily. It is not a sign of being a good writer to show off in this way; quite the opposite.

In *The Complete Plain Words* Gowers quotes the five rules that Fowler gives in *The King's English* for being 'direct, simple, brief, vigorous and lucid':

- prefer the familiar word to the far-fetched;
- prefer the single word to the circumlocution;
- prefer the short word to the long;
- prefer the Saxon word to the Romance;
- prefer the concrete word to the abstract.

Prefer the familiar word to the far-fetched:

If you can write:	*Do not write:*
buy	purchase or acquire
measure	quantify
perhaps	perchance
send	issue
write	communicate

Prefer the short word to the long:

If you can write:	*Do not write:*
hope	expectations
kind	categories
now	currently
repay	reimburse
right	appropriate

Prefer the single word to the circumlocution:

If you can write:	*Do not write:*
act	take action on the issue
often	in several instances
quickly	with the minimum of delay
reconciled	effected a reconciliation
scarce	in short supply
so	with the result that
when	on the occasion when
worth	valued at

Prefer the Saxon word to the Romance. As Fowler says, this rule is the least important, and also the least helpful, because most people do not know the difference between words of Saxon and Romance origin. The Romance languages are those that come directly from Latin: mainly French, Spanish and Italian. We have listed some words that people use, in pairs containing one Saxon and one Romance word. The words in each pair are similar in meaning. This may enable you to feel the differences between the two sources; it should also illustrate how this rule confirms the others.

Saxon	*Romance*
earnings	profit
fall	depreciate
loss	cost
output	production
rise	appreciate, increase
roughly	approximately
show	demonstrate
thought	consideration

Prefer the concrete word to the abstract. Compare these expressions:

transportation facilities	lorries, cars
entrance	door

communications	roads, trains
communication	letter, postcard
providing information	informing
in connection with	about
your attention is drawn	please note
in conjunction with	with
have in possession	possess

In each pair the words ending -tion, -sion, -ilities or -nce are abstract nouns. The wording is simpler and more vigorous if you replace them with concrete (= not abstract) nouns (lorries, cars, door, roads, trains, letter, postcard) or verbs (inform, note, possess) or prepositions (about, with).

The reason for this is that readers can understand more easily what they can 'picture'; their imagination supports their intellect. This is why speakers at a public meeting find visual aids a help, and why (according to the Chinese proverb) one picture is worth a thousand words. An abstract idea is by definition a concept, an idea of the intellect. On the other hand a concrete noun exists in three dimensions and can be photographed. You can photograph a printed word, or a piece of paper containing a word, or a notice board, but you cannot photograph 'information' because it is not that sort of thing. It is abstract.

If your document contains a graph or a picture, the imagination will grasp it for the intellect. If your words contain concrete nouns, such as 'pound coin' or 'factory' or 'car', readers will easily form their own picture; the fact that different readers have different pictures is less important. The imagination can come into play.

Most specialists' writing has to be fairly abstract; it is about assets and liabilities and prospects. Abstract nouns are liable to be ambiguous: 'appreciation' has two distinct meanings; 'delegation' means different things to different people; 'productivity' has emotional force but no commonly accepted meaning until it is defined. Make sure that you define such terms, and beware of the disease which Fowler's *Modern English Usage* calls 'abstractitis', in which a writer becomes addicted to the abstract and becomes unable to write differently. Remember the link between using passive verbs and abstract nouns (see p.31).

If you find yourself saying 'A recommendation is made for the mechanisation to be introduced for the operation acceleration' when you might say 'We recommend a machine to speed up the works', go through your paper and underline every noun ending in -tion, every noun ending in -ility (for they are abstract too), and every passive verb. Then rewrite what you can as concrete and active.

Non-sexism

Language changes continually, and the most difficult aspects to follow are those where we risk offending our readers. This unfortunate word 'non-sexism' is the label of those trying to escape from the traditional English conventions in which masculine terms such as 'he' meant sometimes a male and sometimes a human, male or female. This convention was always ambiguous and is now widely offensive.

There is not yet an agreed set of non-sexist alternatives to traditional usage, but you can change

A Doctor feels that he should have the usual choice of meal.

to: *A Doctor feels that he or she should have the usual choice of meal.*

or: *Doctors feel that they should have the usual choice of meal.*

or: *A Doctor may want the usual choice of meal.*

In other words, either go for the longer version ('he or she'); or the plural 'they'; or recast the sentence more drastically.

Some employers make non-sexist writing compulsory in their house style. All writers must sooner or later come to terms with the real problem, which is exactly which non-sexist term to use, as so many of the alternative terms are ugly, and a book giving many variants is useful (see Appendix 7). We have tried to write this book in a non-sexist way that will, we hope, give little offence either to advocates or to opponents of non-sexism.

The Plain English Campaign

The influence of *The Complete Plain Words* today is obvious in the name of the Plain English Campaign. This campaign is concerned with the design and language of official forms and commercial documents so that those who sign hire-purchase agreements, for example, or insurance policies, should be able to understand what they sign. It is also concerned with the layout, typography and language of government forms, particularly those going to the general public.

Although these documents are not primarily ones with which this book is concerned, the preceding paragraphs on language, layout and style apply to all official writing.

The National Consumer Council has backed the Plain English Campaign because quasi-legal language has long been used in the market-place to baffle or bully consumers.

In *The Complete Plain Words* there has always been a section saying that lawyers cannot be expected to conform to the ideals of the book. But today this view is questionable; there seems no good reason why lawyers should not write plainly, and it would be in the interests of the community that they should try harder to do so than they have in the past. There is even a lawyers' group, called appropriately 'Clarity', applying the ideals of Plain English to legal writing.

Professional language

Much of this section has been devoted to condemning rare words and recommending everyday language. Many writers are not happy with this. They fear that the readers will think that the writer is 'talking down' to them. This fear must be responsible for much of the long-winded language written today. But ask yourself how often in the past you have read documents that were written in such simple language that you felt insulted; and if the answer is 'never', forget about the risk of 'talking down'.

Any form of business, management, profession, or expert activity depends on using technical terms which go against Fowler's rules. When professionals are writing to others in the same profession there is no objection to this. But when they write to non-professionals they should define the technical terms, the jargon, that they cannot avoid using, and the definition should use only everyday language or words already defined. Above all they should avoid those abstract nouns which are not necessary to the professional message.

Chapter 4

Time and Technology

Planning the time

An effective piece of writing must also be cost-effective. The main cost of producing a document will be time, and of that chiefly the time spent by the writer and any superiors who revise the work. All those who intend to be cost-conscious writers should be able to control the time, that is make accurate estimates of how long is reasonable, and minimise the length.

Unfortunately, estimates are difficult to make, and when made are liable to be too low. Moreover the natural differences between individuals and assignments make it dangerous to prescribe any one method of estimating, or establish any standard times.

The first point of importance is that you should look back to your previous work, and see how long you have in fact taken over each job. If you have no idea, then keep a record of the time spent on your next job, and build up an accurate picture of the time allowance needed for each kind of writing.

Break down these estimates to apply to small parts of the job as far as possible. In replying to letters that can be answered with little preliminary thought, which are not long, and which have to be answered on the day received, it is enough to say how many you can write in an hour. At the other end of the size-scale, with long and difficult reports, the job needs to be divided in two ways: first into various chapters or sections, and second into the various stages through which each section must pass.

If deadlines are calculated for each stage, you can see if you are ahead of the target or behind, and establish how to make the next estimate more accurate.

If we look at each stage we see that the cost of producing a long document will depend on:

- the speed with which the writer can sort ideas into relevant and irrelevant; Chapter 1 covers this;

- the efficiency with which writers can arrange sections under convenient headings and into a suitable order; see Chapter 2;
- their speed and efficiency in drafting the text, the time lost by interruptions and whether they can use dictating machines or word processors;
- the back-up service provided by the organisation in turning a draft into a finished document;
- the amount of work a writer can perform automatically, by following precedent, or a house style guide, or other standards;
- the time allowed for revision;
- the time necessary for editing by a superior, and then the author's re-writing (see Chapter 5).

Where to write

Choose a working environment suitable for swift and effective writing. Some people work best in a busy office with background noise; some like background music; others need peace and quiet to concentrate. Try different places and methods. Most employers seem to expect their staff to work in offices where interruptions and distractions are at their worst. Those who prefer quiet, and work more effectively with long periods free from interruption, might consider these suggestions:

- in the office of an absent colleague;
- in a public library;
- in a parked car;
- in a train;
- at home;
- in an office set aside for concentrated writing, either on the premises of their own employer, or on a client's premises.

Sometimes modern technology provides an answer. Telephone calls can be re-routed. Answering machines on each extension, or some similar device for storing messages, cut down wasted time. Headphone stereos cut down distracting noise.

An employer who forces staff not only to stay at their desks, but to answer the telephone (for example, to provide a service to customers or the public), must expect the time, and therefore cost, of writing at least to double.

Those who know 'flexitime' know that they can write twice

as efficiently at the beginning or end of the day as in the 'core time' simply because there are fewer interruptions.

The writer is totally inaccessible in a train or in a parked car (except to anyone who knows the parking place). In the other places there is much less risk of being disturbed by the telephone. However, in some places it is not easy to ensure that all the relevant papers will be accessible. The range of places where people can write effectively is wider if they use dictating machines properly; for which see the following paragraphs.

Dictating machines

Compared with shorthand, the advantages of dictating machines are:

- the range of times and places for dictating is wider;
- they save the expensive time of the shorthand writer.

However, there is a disadvantage:

- the author and typist are separated, and so cannot ask questions as they go, acting immediately on the answers. Feedback is delayed. This disadvantage is reduced if the dictator and audio-typist meet and discuss the work, each having sympathy for the other's problems.

Compared with longhand, the advantages of dictating machines are:

- with practice, the author can draft the text more swiftly and in more places;
- typists usually understand the spoken word more easily than the handwritten.

However, there are two disadvantages:

- some difficult thinking can be done by writing a draft in longhand; with dictating machines, the basic thinking should be done first;
- it is difficult to dictate tables of figures, except the simplest.

Before dictating the text, say:

- who you are;
- how long the document is;
- what kind of document it is: letter, memo, etc;
- what size of paper is needed;
- how many copies;
- when the document must be ready by;
- to whom it is addressed.

In most dictating machine systems, much of this information can be conveyed on a covering slip of paper sent to the typist with the dictating tape. The typist needs to see the incoming letter when typing the reply, and other papers referred to in the text of the dictation. This saves trying to say it all in the machine.

During dictation

- be friendly to the typist; put in a bit of the background to make the job more interesting; say if it will be easy and apologise if it will be difficult; compensate where possible for the impersonal nature of audio-typing.
- be careful with lists. If the list is long, leave the numbering to the typist once you have started the series off. For complex work, enclose a draft layout.
- put in any punctuation, spelling, or underlining, and all paragraphing, unless you have some other understanding with the typist. The typist may spell better than the dictator, but the dictator is probably better placed to spell the names of people and places and technical terms; and at the end of the day it is all the dictator's responsibility.
- do not mumble.
- do not rush, and do not let the machine run on while you are thinking what comes next. Use the 'Stop' button.
- many typists will listen and type alternately. Therefore dictate in meaningful phrases of four or five words that can be easily remembered.
- hold the microphone the proper distance from your mouth and nose according to the manufacturer's instructions.
- use a natural voice, with some expression, as though talking, not reading.
- unless it is a rough draft, play back what you have dictated. When you are learning to use the machine, play back everything carefully before sending it for typing.

A typing pool (as compared with individual typists for individual dictators) has these advantages:

- lower cost: a pool is normally large enough with only one typist for ten dictators;
- fewer bottlenecks: work load is evened out between typists;

but has these disadvantages:

- there is less understanding between author and typist, and so less job satisfaction;

- the typist is apt to approach each piece of work without knowledge of the background, and so is more likely to make a mistake.

An organisation, and dictators themselves, can minimise these disadvantages by:

- trying to arrange for the same typist to deal with all work from the same dictator, except in an emergency;
- dictators showing that they are aware of the typist's isolated role, and the problems it brings;
- dictators meeting typists when possible, to talk about current work, to be friendly, to thank them, and listen to their advice on how to improve their dictation.

Word processors

Another valuable help in writing is the computer, particularly in the form usually called a word processor.

Traditionally there have been executives who wrote, often highly educated individuals, usually men, and those who typed and did secretarial work, nearly always women. Many still argue that it is not efficient to use the highly paid time of an executive to do what they see as typists' work.

On the other hand, typing is easier than driving a car, and if 'status' is the barrier, those who cannot type on a computer keyboard will slowly lose power to those who have no inhibitions about it, including most school-leavers, who now have got used to working through keyboards.

With the development of home computers, and the fall in price of word processors, many executives are discovering the advantages of using a keyboard themselves. Some of these advantages are:

1. Neat writing appears on the screen; much easier to follow, and more flattering, than scrawled manuscript. As you can see what you have written before it is printed, you do not have to be a good typist to produce good typing.
2. The writer can plan the structure first, putting down points or headings, and then exploit the machine's device by which new writing appears where needed, pushing apart what has been written to make room.
3. The writer can see two or three versions of the same

sentence or paragraph on the screen simultaneously, before deciding which one to use.

4. If the sequence of sections is wrong, the text can be moved around in chunks.
5. Writers can hop about from end to end of a document, without the awkwardness of handling several papers at once.
6. Those frequently writing letters which are similar but not identical, for example answers to enquiries, can call up the previous answer from a disc, remember points which might otherwise have been overlooked, and make adjustments of tone or content which might be difficult for anyone else to make. It may help to have one master answer containing all possible sentences, so that all the writers have to do is 'rub out', which is much easier and neater on a word processor than on a written document.
7. One whole operation, typing, is in effect saved. The letter once written electronically can be typed automatically. The saving in time may be enough to justify the machine.
8. Word processing is not the only use of computers for writers. As the computer calculates easily, letters can incorporate forward estimates, work out actual costs as a percentage of forecast, re-forecast, and print the result as a histogram or graph in a way that would previously have required an art department.
9. The computer's power of selection makes it possible to develop management by exception, or other logical work, where what goes into a document depends on the result of a computer calculation.
10. Filing is more compact, and documents more quickly retrieved and read, than by using a filing cabinet.

There are drawbacks. The machines have to be kept in their place, and this technology is advancing more rapidly than humans can perhaps adapt, or be trained, to use it.

- *Do not be long-winded.* It is easy to say too much where you can summon a sentence or paragraph at the press of a button.
- *Do not repeat yourself.* It is not good to summon up the same 'chunk' twice in a letter; to have obviously word-processed passages, even in different letters to the same reader, does not make a good impression.

- *Do not go through innumerable drafts.* Where the typing pool use word processors, writers have to understand the difficulties of the pool as with dictating machines. It makes no sense to put a document through ten drafts in the misguided belief that if there are only a few small alterations each time it costs nothing. Normally, even for a long and important document, discipline yourself to a limit of one rough draft for editing before you have the fair copy printed.

Checking and revising

Why?

Many working documents are written by someone to whom the job has been delegated; it has then to go out with the authority of the section, department, or of the whole organisation. Such delegated writing is edited by a superior, and Chapter 5 discusses the way of doing this. Apart from such editing, authors should check their own writing. It is quick, enjoyable, and of great value. Most writers, skilled or unskilled, find that they can make great improvements between first and second drafts.

Where?

Choose a place for revising the draft as carefully as for writing it. However, revising is more likely to require a desk than writing the first draft using a dictating machine, particularly as you may need access to your notes, and to the books recommended in the Bibliography.

When?

The method of writing determines the time of revising:

- handwritten: read it through before you send it off.
- copy-typed: read it before you send it for typing, and again after it comes back.
- shorthand: either have it read back from the shorthand before it is typed, or have a rough draft typed and revise that.
- dictating machine: play back a short document, and have a rough draft of a long document.

Who?

First, the writer. Always check your own writing. But unless the document is unimportant, invite someone else to check through what you are sending after you have checked it. Choose an equal, if possible; differences of status sometimes inhibit criticism. Try to choose someone who knows as much about the subject as your readers but not much more.

How?

You can hardly check the draft against all the points discussed in this book. But with experience, you will discover your own strengths and weaknesses and the particular problems of your kind of work and your readers, and you will be able to compile your own checklist. Meanwhile, try this list of questions:

- Will the document make a good first impression? Is it better than the reader was expecting? It should be.
- Will it be easy to find quickly the answers to the questions uppermost in the reader's mind? If some of these questions are not answered, can the reader find out quickly why not?
- Is there a statement of purpose or terms of reference? Can the reader see how far these have been answered?
- If the reader reads the headings by themselves, or the table of contents if there is one, is it clear where to find any given point? Does the text under each heading contain what the heading led the reader to expect?
- Can readers use the headings and numberings to refer quickly to any one short passage at subsequent meetings or in letters?
- Is the meaning clear and unambiguous?
- Are there fewer than ten lines, or three sentences, a paragraph, on average?
- Are there on average fewer than 40 words a sentence?
- Does it sound confident without being arrogant?

The answers should, so far, be 'Yes'. Now for questions to which the answer should be 'No':

- Are there rare words where familiar words would do instead?
- Are there abstract nouns, where verbs or concrete nouns would serve?
- Are there long words where short ones would be as good?
- Are there long phrases where one word would serve?
- Are there passive verbs where the active would serve?
- Are there adjectives, where a verb, or nothing, would do instead?

- Will the reader have to read any passages twice?
- Is it monotonous?
- Does it assume knowledge, or attitudes, or values, that the readers may not share?

Chapter 5

Editing Reports

Methods of editing

Editing the reports of subordinates is a part of a senior manager's role. As the superior, the editor is responsible for seeing the report does credit to the section, firm, or profession. But that is not the only reason for careful editing. As a manager, the senior man is responsible for training subordinates; this must include improving their skills, which include the skill of writing. The good editor will use editing as an opportunity to train staff as well as to improve that particular document.

Too often, editors merely duplicate the work of writers. Under pressure of time, they ignore the training aspect. Editing in this way can be counter-productive; it lowers the morale of the subordinate whose draft is edited, and whose next piece of writing may be worse. Writers see no point in perfecting a document if whatever they write is rewritten.

Editors may rewrite the document to the standard the client requires, or, in an organisation with many levels of management, to the standards other senior levels require. They may fail to discuss these standards with the original writer, and not explain what was wrong with the first version, or discuss the changes they have introduced.

All the original writers know is that a document written with some care has been rewritten. Naturally they take this as a criticism. As they are not given the opportunity to discuss the changes, they can only guess at what was wrong with their version. They may try to do better next time, and succeed. They may try but guess wrongly what was the matter with the earlier draft, and do even worse. Or they may feel that if the draft is going to be rewritten by superiors, there is no point in spending much effort on it. So next time the editor has even more rewriting to do. It is bad enough to keep a dog and bark yourself; but here the more you bark, the less the dog will bother.

Editing as training

The editor should take the draft report or other document, and instead of rewriting the parts that need it, should note these passages, and indicate what is the objection to them in their present form. The writer then does the actual rewording. This has three advantages:

- it saves the editor time;
- it results in a document in one style, rather than a patchwork from different hands;
- it enables the editor to see from the reworded version that the writer has grasped the point of the criticism.

If editing is to be good training, it must have a basis in criteria which are objective, pre-agreed, and logical, such as:

- a specified dictionary, for correct spelling and meaning;
- specified authorities on English style, such as those in the Bibliography of this book;
- a 'house style' handbook or guide, to cover whatever standards and principles the organisation applies to give quality and consistency to their documents.

As well as these criteria which apply to every document, there are criteria for editing which are special for each case. These too should be pre-agreed, so that the writer does not start off on the wrong lines, and when the document is edited to meet these criteria, there is no legitimate grievance.

The main 'special criteria' should be stated in the Terms of Reference (see pp.15-17); if they are adequate and in writing, all should be well.

However, there may be matters which cannot be put in writing, either because they are too secret, or because they involve questions of (for example) personality, politics, prejudice, or culture. These are better communicated face to face because they are subtle and require an interchange of question and answer. Therefore there must be a preliminary interview between superior and subordinate. Such an interview will mean less editing later, and better training and satisfaction for the writer.

The editing interview

The editor and writer should meet to discuss the first typed draft. This meeting has three objectives:

- to improve the document under discussion;
- to improve the writer's understanding of what makes a working document good or bad;
- to check that the writer is receiving good enough support from the organisation, including guidance on what standards the organisation expects, enough time for writing, a suitable place, and proper clerical service.

Before the interview begins, the editor should:
- check that there are available such reference books as a dictionary and Fowler's *Modern English Usage*;
- read the draft;
- note points where improvement is needed, and what is the objection to the writer's version, without rewriting; if it is essential to rewrite to make the point, produce more than one acceptable version;
- assess the writer's progress by comparing this draft with others from the same writer;
- plan the interview.

The plan or agenda for the interview need not necessarily follow the outline below, but this may serve as an example:
- welcome and thank the writer; establish 'rapport';
- give an overall impression of the document;
- answer any questions the writer wants to raise, or any special difficulty which arose in writing the document;
- discuss one by one the points where an improvement is worth making;
- on each point obtain the writer's rewording and amend the draft accordingly;
- if possible, say the document will go forward for issue as amended;
- if necessary, ask the writer to take the document away for redrafting to meet the objections discussed; and arrange a date for another editing interview;
- check that the writer has received the support and service needed or expected;
- if necessary, discuss training;
- sum up, repeat thanks, and express confidence.

After the interview, the editor should check its results against objectives, following up any action points from the interview. It will help to consider whether the amount of editing required for this writer is rising or falling, and refer to this at the next progress interview; and whether the writer is writing more quickly and effectively as a result of editorial guidance.

Cost-effective editing

The cost of editing is time, multiplied by the cost of the time. As editors tend to be busier than their subordinates, engaged on more important work, and their time is more expensive, it is important for the editor to do as little editing as possible, and it is economical to achieve this by transferring the load where possible to the writer or the writer's colleagues.

The methods outlined above should be cost-effective because:

- by agreeing on objective criteria, less time is spent arguing about what is wrong and why;
- the editor is likely to alter less if all changes have to be explained, rather than just made without explanation;
- time spent rewriting is transferred from superior to subordinate;
- if editing is also good training, the skills of the subordinate will improve in time, so reducing the amount of editing needed.

There are difficulties in the way of this policy:

- few firms have house style guides;
- the editor may often 'feel' a passage is wrong, but not know how to explain it except by rewriting;
- as time may be short and editors and writers are both away from the office for long periods, it may be impossible to arrange the meetings that the policy requires.

These difficulties, however, should be overcome. If the document has to go out immediately, the editing discussion should follow as soon as possible afterwards. Poor editing means that documents issued will be of high cost and low quality; and staff who are not trained on the job as outlined above, may well continue to believe that the number of corrections made to their drafts depends less on whether they have done a good job than on how much time their superior has to spare. The question is not only of cost and quality, but also of motivation and morale.

Part 2. Particular Applications

Chapter 6

Reports

Kinds of report

The basic routine for writing reports consists of collecting information, analysing it and then reporting it to others. Industry, commerce, and the professions depend on reports.

The form of a report can vary considerably, from a telephone call to a long formal report. As spoken reporting is outside the scope of this book, and Chapter 7 considers short letters and memoranda, this chapter is concerned only with those longer documents usually called 'reports'.

We first consider certain basic principles common to all report writing; second, we state the special characteristics of routine reports and non-routine reports; and third, we distinguish between external and internal non-routine reports. Finally, we consider some special cases such as an engineer's report and an accountant's report.

The distinction between routine and non-routine reports can be illustrated by these examples:

- a monthly financial statement sent to divisional general management would be an example of a routine report;
- an accident report would be an example of a non-routine report.

Common features

Most reports are likely to share the following common features, regardless of other differences:

- *Formal structure and tone.* Reports tend to be more formal than other sorts of communication. They usually have a more structured format, possibly involving a title page, summary, table of contents, introduction, conclusions, list of recommendations, and appendices. They avoid niceties of address, and are normally more impersonal, with no extraneous conversational content. A report format is therefore particularly suitable for documents which are to have a wide circulation or to be kept for posterity.

- *Pictorial presentation.* The use of pictures, graphs, diagrams etc. is increasing because it makes numerical information easier to understand. Chapter 9 considers the forms of pictorial presentation more fully.
- *Statement of opinion.* In most reports the writer draws conclusions after marshalling, reviewing, and evaluating the evidence. Because these conclusions are likely to be fundamental to the purpose of the report, the report writer needs to be particularly certain about the factual accuracy of the supporting evidence.
- *'Use' of the report.* Whatever the type of report, it will only succeed as a piece of effective writing if the writer has a clear understanding of the needs of the readers, and puts in the report what is relevant to those needs.

Routine reports

Normally routine reports are internal, and have the characteristics noted below.

Regular format

Because they are routine these reports can be produced as standardised forms with boxes to complete. This makes both writing and reading the report quicker and easier, since both writers and readers are familiar with the layout. The forms can be designed so as to highlight exceptional circumstances, and permit comment on these by the writer. There is a corresponding risk, however, that the habit of the routine might result in the form not being adapted to meet the changing needs of the users (readers). A typical example of a routine report to management might be the monthly and cumulative turnover figures, analysed by product and selling region. These could be presented as graphs or tables, with provision for comments and for highlighting unexpected results. See Appendix 4 for an example.

Terms of reference

Because it is unlikely that terms of reference will be repeated on each report, there will be no statement of objective against which the report's continued usefulness can be measured, so increasing the risk mentioned in *Defining the terms*, p.15. 'We have always done it that way' is the excuse for much useless writing and wasted time. To safeguard against this the writer should periodically ask readers whether the report is still useful to them, whether they want other information, and whether there is any current information which they no longer need.

Knowledge of the readers

The writer is likely to know the readers well; and anyway should have little difficulty in getting to know them. As Chapter 1 states, knowing the readers assists in determining style, method of presentation, what is likely to be relevant and so on.

Feedback

Because of the regularity of the report the writer will probably get feedback from the users and other sources. This should also help in producing a more effectively written report.

Headings

Because of the use of a standardised form of report, the usual headings, Introduction, Conclusion, Recommendations etc. will not necessarily apply.

Style

Because much of the report will consist of pictorial matter the question of style may be limited to choosing the best method of laying out the figures and the verbal style of any comments. It can be acceptable to ignore grammatical rules; thus a routine report might say 'Deficit caused by strike at suppliers' where this would not be acceptable in a report to another organisation.

Top data

A typical routine report might be headed with the following information:

- name of author
- title of document
- date of period covered
- date of issue
- distribution and confidentiality
- reference numbers

Confidentiality

Confidentiality can pose a serious problem for the writer if the report has a wide distribution, particularly to employees at different levels. The writer has to know what is confidential, to whom, and until when. The Access to Information Act has made this a serious matter for local authorities, but any writer must omit from the report anything that should not be passed to any of the recipients; sensitive facts needed by certain of the recipients can be supplied by supplementary reports.

Non-routine reports

Non-routine reports are by definition specially commissioned, for a specific, usually single, purpose. Most non-routine reports, whether internal or external, should have the following characteristics.

Terms of reference

The writer will need to establish agreed written terms of reference, at a preliminary meeting, before planning the investigation. As we have said, effective writing requires the author to understand clearly the use of the document to the reader. With non-routine reports this is particularly important since there will be no previous guidelines and no feedback. Similarly, it is unlikely that a standardised form can be used, as it can with routine reports; therefore each report has to be viewed as a 'one-off' assignment and treated on its merits.

Investigative approach

In detail this will vary according to the subject matter of the report. However, the broad approach is likely to be similar in each case, as follows:

- Having obtained the terms of reference, the investigator collects evidence, taking comprehensive notes and recording the sources. Writers should constantly check their notes for relevance to the purpose of the investigation; and consider whether relevant facts or areas of investigation have escaped scrutiny.
- Once the evidence is reasonably complete the investigator should review and sift it in the light of the purpose, and should double check important facts and sources. It may be possible at this stage to form preliminary conclusions.

- The investigator should discuss with the readers the facts ascertained, and conclusions and recommendations, before drafting the final form of the report. This allows for further work if necessary, and for reconsideration; and enables the writer to draft the report knowing the likely reaction of the recipients.
- Where limits are placed on the investigator's freedom of action, or it has been impossible to reach a firm opinion, the report should explain the details.

Layout

A typical layout might consist of the following:

- *Title page.* This gives the author's name, organisation, and reference; the title of the report; the date of issue (month and year may be enough); and the name or reference of the person or organisation being addressed.
- *Summary.* This is only necessary for a long report. It gives a 'bird's eye view' of the whole report, summarising the background to the investigation, the investigative work conducted, and the main conclusions and recommendations.
- *Table of contents.* This is also only needed in a long report. It should list, in order, all the headings, including Appendices, with the page on which each is found, and either section numbering or paragraph numbering, or both.
- *Introduction.* This would include in outline the background history that led to the report being commissioned, the terms of reference, a brief account of the method of investigation, and acknowledgements of help received.
- *The evidence.* This should be arranged under different sections and headings for easier reference and understanding. The structure and headings chosen will depend on the subject matter of the report, but should present the reader with a succinct indication of the text that follows. As an example, the following structure might apply to a long-term report to an issuing house:

  History and development of the business
  Outline of current operations
  Premises and plant
  Management and other staff
  Trading results (possibly tabulated or pictorial)
  Net assets

Capital employed
Prospects (based on management's representations)
Appendices

- *Conclusions.* There is no reason against these being written as essay-type prose, but if there are several conclusions they are best listed and numbered. Conclusions and Recommendations normally come at the end of the report, which is logical for the writer. However, the word 'conclusions' does not mean that they come at the end; it means that they are the judgement after reasoned argument about the evidence.

  If the important readers are likely to read them first, or perhaps not to refer to the evidence at all, it might be sensible for Conclusions and Recommendations to come at the beginning, before the detailed evidence on which they are based.

  If the report has a summary, this will mention the main conclusions; if there is no summary, it may be convenient to have a summary of the conclusions at the beginning and the full conclusions at the end. Where the writer knows that the decisions will be taken by more senior officials than those to whom the report is going directly, it might be useful to prepare a separate statement of Conclusions and Recommendations.
- *Recommendations.* See 'Conclusions' above. Recommendations should appear as a list, which if long, should be suitably subdivided into sections. Avoid using the term 'Summary of Recommendations' except for a condensed list, not a complete list. Under this heading, it should not be necessary to present arguments to justify the recommendations; that should have been done under 'Conclusions', from which the recommendations should logically follow.
- *Appendices.* These are useful in a long report, to reduce the bulk of the evidence sections. They should also contain any technical evidence which some readers will find unintelligible or will want to miss out. There can be as many appendices as necessary, and each one can be as long as is appropriate. There is no objection to the appendices being longer than the rest of the report.

Engineering and science reports

Structure

An *à la carte* menu for the structure of these reports might be:

- Title page
- Summary (abstract)
- Table of Contents (including appendices)
- Introduction
- Theory
- Experimental Procedure and Results
- Discussion
- Conclusions
- Recommendations
- Acknowledgements
- List of References
- Appendices
  - Tables, illustrations, graphs
  - Literature survey
  - Bibliography
  - Glossary and list of abbreviations, signs and symbols
- Index
- Distribution list

Most of these headings mean what has been described above (pp.58-9). Some others will be clear enough to the writers. There are a few points of difficulty or wider interest.

Keywords

Scientists and engineers have been quicker than others to exploit the value of having special words (keywords) which can be used in a computer database to identify the scope of the report for electronic retrieval. The words of the title are seldom as satisfactory for this as words chosen by the author for the purpose. Sometimes the keywords are in a section on the front cover, sometimes after the distribution list at the end.

Discussion and Conclusion

The Discussion is where the author comments on the evidence in the previous sections, and indicates the value of the main facts discovered. It may be a long section. The Conclusion is short, often only one sentence, giving the final answer to the problem stated in the introduction. The Discussion may correspond roughly to the judge's summing up in a trial, where the Conclusion corresponds to the jury's verdict. Others outside science and engineering could distinguish in the same way, but as authors are both judge and jury in their own report, most non-technical writers find it convenient to unite these parts under the heading 'Conclusion'.

References and Bibliography
The difference between these is that the References are sources mentioned in the body of the report, whereas the Bibliography should be further reading not so mentioned.

Reports to public authorities

Local authorities and health authorities are run by unpaid individuals, appointed or elected from the public, who have to take decisions based on reports submitted by full-time officers. The full council mainly delegates decisions to committees, but such committees may have agendas of 200 pages to read before each meeting, mostly reports. It follows that the reports have to be of a high standard, in a plain style, concise and well structured. Many local authorities have a house style document governing the structure of their reports.

The main difference between the structure of such reports and others is that commonly the committees or authorities require the Recommendations (which may be called Proposals or some other name) at the front of the report rather than at the back. The chief reason for this is that it enables busy committee members to decide quickly whether they need to read any further. The wording is usually prescribed, so that if the meeting accepts the recommendations, a few simple changes to the agenda through a word processor provide the minutes.

Appendix 3.2 gives a sample short report for such an authority.

External non-routine reports

Examples of such reports would include consultant reports, some visit reports, investigations into fraud, the proposed sale or purchase of a business, an application for government aid, or the issue of a prospectus to shareholders. The form and content are likely to be determined by the kind of report, by the readers and purposes as usual, and possibly by legal, professional, or conventional requirements. In addition to the points made under Non-routine reports, pp.56-8, the following four special matters affect external reports.

Terms of reference
These are particularly important and must be comprehensive. They form the basis of the whole investigation and report. As they form a kind of contract, they should be in writing, possibly in a letter such as a Letter of Engagement. If they are modified this should be recorded in the Introduction to the report. The writer is likely to be less familiar with the readers than for a routine report, so the prior discussions are important in clarifying the purposes of the report.

Prior discussions
It is particularly important that the writer be involved in discussions before starting the investigation. There will be little feedback or 'grapevine' information. If writers have a discussion with the readers before the final draft is written, they can clear contentious or uncertain points, gauge their likely reactions to the findings, and decide on the most effective form of presentation.

Presentation
This merits close attention, at least for the reason that the report may be all that the client sees for the fee. The points in pp.45-6 apply here, and in particular:

- use simple and concise language
- avoid unnecessary technical jargon
- leave no room for ambiguity in the Conclusions and Recommendations
- edit the document to eliminate any discrepancies, inconsistencies of style, or other blemishes.

Formality
All reports are comparatively formal, and external reports are particularly so. They should be formally addressed, and the tone of writing should be official, with particular attention to correct grammar and usage.

Internal non-routine reports

These reports might be, for example, about changes in an organisation, or the effects of some external developments upon it. Subjects could include marketing, buying policy, redesign of product, new production methods, or cost variances. The comments on non-routine reports on pp.56-8 apply here, together with the three aspects listed below which relate to internal reports.

Terms of reference

Although the writer still needs terms of reference, they will often be less well defined by the originators of the report, and the writer may well have to submit a redefinition to the originators for approval. The writer will, however, benefit from greater familiarity with the readers, and will probably obtain some feedback as the investigation proceeds. So written terms of reference are less critical than for an external report.

Presentation

There is likely to be a little difference in investigative method between external and internal reports. But in presenting the internal report the layout is more likely to be influenced by the firm's guidelines or house rules, and brevity may become rather more important with courtesy slightly less so. The writer should always consider the needs of the ultimate user.

Preliminary thinking

Before starting the investigation, the writer should answer the following questions:

- Is a written report really necessary? Why would a telephone call or discussion not be sufficient?
- What use will the reader want to make of the report? What will the reader have to decide? How can the report be undertaken and written to make these things easier for the readers?
- If the information is to be passed on, who are the ultimate readers, and what are their requirements likely to be? What form, presentation and language will they be most likely to appreciate?
- Will the originator have to use the report to convince others? If so, how can the report be best prepared to help? What will appear relevant to these other people? Writers have to consider factors which the readers think are important, even if the readers are wrong.
- Is a written report needed for the files, for posterity? This is not useless, and is less vague than it sounds; it means

the report is to help another person deal with a connected problem at a later date.

- What variety of presentation can be used (tables, graphs, diagrams)?
- Is there likely to be a problem of confidentiality?

The post-audit management letter

The post-audit management letter is considered in this chapter because, although the opening and closing formalities are those of a letter, in all other respects it has the qualities of a report. You should refer to Chapter 7 for discussion of the opening and closing formalities.

It is unlike other reports, in that

- it is not specially commissioned, except in so far as it may be commissioned by the letter of engagement;
- it does not involve any special investigation, but is a by-product of the work carried out primarily for auditing the accounts.

The purpose of the post-audit management letter

As a piece of effective writing, it has two purposes:

- to persuade management to alter the existing accounting system where needed, so as to correct weaknesses, reduce the risk of fraud, save costs and delay, and generally increase efficiency;
- to provide a record of recommendations made as a defence against later accusations of negligence.

To meet the first purpose, the report must satisfy these points:

- The tone should be sympathetic, persuasive, and constructive. If the Letter is simply a catalogue of faults, its unrelieved gloom is apt to be counter-productive. Rather than emphasise what is wrong at present, emphasise the improvements that can be made, the advantages of making them, and perhaps the reasons why a method appropriate in the past is so no longer.
- The criticisms should be specific, detailed, and factual, and the corresponding recommendations should be practical, always considering the size and resources of the client organisation.
- Make clear the relative importance of different weaknesses, and avoid trivia that will detract from the serious points and annoy readers.

- Collecting information and drafting points for inclusion in the Letter should not be left until the end of the audit; it should begin from the beginning of the audit. As each section of the audit is completed the points can be reviewed and transferred to a main schedule from which the draft Letter will be written, and which will form the basis of the discussion with the client.
- Submit the Letter as early as possible, both for courtesy and for action. Corrective action is more probable the sooner the matter is discussed after discovery. Delay implies a lack of urgency. Matters are more likely to be fresh in the minds of both auditor and client if discussion follows quickly on discovery and report follows quickly on discussion. If the report is submitted after an interim audit, action may be possible before the year-end, and so influence the final audit opinion.
- Send it to the main board or to a member of the main board. First, because they are ultimately responsible for the proper conduct of business, and should have an opportunity to assess its shortcomings and consider opportunities for improvement. Second, because the report may imply criticism of some members of management, who should not have the chance of suppressing significant information. In practice a short report may sometimes be sent to the directors and the full report to the chief accountant.
- Writing and submitting the Management Letter should only be the first stage in a continuous process of recommendation, action, and follow-up.

To meet the second purpose, the report should:

- include a record of all the significant matter that arose during the audit, with related recommendations. The audit file should contain full details of any errors found so that comments made in the Letter may be substantiated.
- comment on each matter in enough detail to leave no doubt about the auditor's view of its importance.
- express recommendations without the chance of ambiguity, doubt, or uncertainty.
- where appropriate, express clearly the risk of fraud or loss in the future.

Discussion with the client

The auditor needs to collect information carefully, making notes that will be useful in discussion with the client and in drafting the report. This review of data is the time to check the factual accuracy of significant points, and arrange them into separate items for discussion with the client and subsequent incorporation in the formal Letter. The discussion with the client should deal with these points, including any corrective action needed, and other matters which can be corrected at once and omitted from the formal Letter. Such a preliminary discussion has these advantages:

- it paves the way for the recommendations.
- it lessens the impact of the eventual criticisms in the Letter.
- it enables the writer to adapt the tone and emphasis of the Letter in the light of the client's first reaction.
- it enables the auditor to avoid mistakes and misapprehensions which would otherwise undermine the credibility of the formal Letter.

Structure

In the investigation report, the conclusions pass judgement on the evidence, and the recommendations are drawn from the conclusions. This applies too to the post-audit letter; but now there are many items, each with separate evidence, conclusions, and recommendations, and perhaps no particular unity.

The structure of a typical post-audit letter might be, in outline:

- Introduction
- Conclusions and recommendations
- Main weaknesses one by one, with comments and recommendations attached to each
- Matters raised in previous Letters, not yet attended to
- Other advice
- Closing formalities.

The introduction in detail could consist of:

- Opening formalities
- Reference to audit work and its purpose
- 'Caveat' that this report was not necessarily an exhaustive list of important weaknesses, but merely those that came up in the course of the audit
- Reference to having discussed the main points already.

The conclusions and recommendations could be an exhaustive recapitulation of those points taken from the central section of the report. If these are the points that the senior members of the client organisation will read first, there is a case for listing them in a covering letter.

The weaknesses should be arranged in some logical order for the reader; this is unlikely to be the order in which the writer made the observations. The classification used for the accounts would be a logical basis for the evidence sections.

For many purposes numbering is useful, and in a long report or management letter it is essential. Each point or item should have a separate paragraph (or several), with a heading, and if appropriate sub-headings, structured to distinguish:

- the observed facts
- the weaknesses arising from the facts
- recommendations and assessment of the costs and savings of implementation.

A suggested structure for each point is:

• Heading of weakness or error	Heading
• Circumstances of weakness or error	
• Company procedure	Facts
• Cause of weakness or error	
• Possible effect of weakness or error	Conclusion
• Recommendations	
• Acceptability of these to client's staff	Recommendations

An alternative columnar format, which has the advantage of preserving this sequence and yet more clearly differentiating between weaknesses and recommendations, and so highlighting the recommendations, is illustrated below. This sets out:

on the left, the circumstances and cause of the weakness or error;

in the centre, the recommendations, costs, and savings, and whether acceptable;

on the right, action proposed by the client, with comments.

• Circumstances of weakness	• Recommend-ation	• Client's reaction to recommendation
• Company procedure	• Acceptability to client's staff	• Subsequent follow-up
• Cause of weakness		
• Possible effect of weakness		

These two methods of layout are illustrated in Appendix 3.

The concluding paragraph should normally contain an expression of appreciation for the assistance given to the auditors by the client's staff, and an offer of further assistance or discussion from the auditors on points made in the Letter. It is sensible to ask for a reply to the Letter, indicating what action the client has taken or intends to take.

Chapter 7

Letters and Memoranda

Efficiency plus politeness

Writing letters and memoranda is a vital part of the desk-worker's skill. Good writers can compose letters swiftly. Their letters are good ambassadors for themselves and their organisation; they are short, clear and civil; they do the job the writers intend, and enable the readers to do *their* job better.

There are many conventions in writing letters and memoranda, and we can begin with the distinction between them. Letters are for those in a different organisation, or those in the same organisation on special occasions (such as a letter of appointment). A memorandum is for someone in the same organisation though not necessarily the same locality. Therefore letters emphasise courtesy and memoranda emphasise efficiency.

A letter is usually typed on paper of a better quality than a memorandum, and with a smarter letterhead. Letters conform to national customs, beginning 'Dear ...' and ending 'Yours ...'; memoranda conform to the rules of the organisation, and usually omit 'Dear' and 'Yours'. Letters are signed at the end; memoranda say who the writer is at the beginning. We have given an example of a letter on p.72 and a memorandum on pp.76-7.

Letter-writers have to be efficient and polite at the same time. This is the first difficulty, because efficiency requires speed of output, but politeness requires that you indicate that you have taken some trouble with the letter. Standard phrases have great advantages: they meet such recurring needs as thanking, asking, promising; they can be carefully drafted once, to be unambiguous, legally correct, and polite; and then they can be used repeatedly without further thought. But there is a kind of discourtesy in any standard phrase, however polite it may be, in that it is apt to sound impersonal; and it is useful to modify the standard phrase to give a better impression.

One example can show how the 'standard phrase' can be modified. The most useful, frequent, polite, and efficient phrase is the opening one to many letters: 'Thank you for your letter of . . .' This can be modified by adding another clause: '. . . about the increase in rent'. Or a clause can be put at the beginning instead of the end: 'We have been concerned about the rent, and must thank you for your letter of . . . about it.' But the most useful variation is to put an additional word (or possibly a phrase) in the middle of the standard phrase: 'Thank you for your interesting letter of . . .' The following diagram shows how the standard phrase may be varied without great thought; but obviously the more of the writer's own personality introduced into the writing the better such writing will be received:

<table>
<tr><td>Thank you
I thank you
We thank you
Many thanks</td><td>for your</td><td>interesting
long
welcome</td><td>letter</td><td>of
dated</td><td>1st January</td></tr>
</table>

As with other effective writing, it is important to be clear what you expect the readers to do on receiving the letter. You can then write to enable and encourage them to do it. Courtesy requires you to put yourself in your reader's place; imagine receiving the letter, looking at it, reading it, thinking about it, acting on it, and filing it. Write so that readers can do all those easily. Do not, for instance, write one letter on two subjects that they will need to file in two places; write two letters, even though they are to the same person on the same day.

Use polite appeals to urge readers to act before you resort to accusing or threatening. Assume that they have overlooked something, or do not understand, before you assume that they have rejected your proposal, or do not care.

Specimen structures

A simple letter or memorandum consists of two parts:

- facts
- action needed.

These two parts may be two paragraphs, or two sentences in the same paragraph, or even two halves of one sentence, as in 'The securities arrived this morning and await your collection.'

In the paragraphs that follow it will be convenient to talk

about the 'points' in a letter or memorandum. The example just given is of a two-point letter; planning a letter means arranging the points.

In deciding the proper structure of a letter there is no need to settle the precise length of each point, and usually no need to give the point a heading in the document. Although the letter or memorandum itself should have a heading, sub-headings should only be required in a complicated memorandum, where they do sometimes help the reader to follow the message. In a short letter sub-headings are not customary.

Simple request

- Facts: I need to examine the projected cash flow for the next three months.
- Action: Please suggest a date and time for the examination.

Complex request

- Facts:
  – who I am
  – what problem has arisen
  – possible solutions
  – reasons against certain solutions
  – the best solution
- Action:
  – A.B. to do this
  – X.Y. to do that.

This sequence resembles the basic outline of a report: problem or purpose; evidence; conclusions; recommendation.

Simple answer to simple request

- Thanks: Thank you for your letter of . . ..
- Response: I suggest we meet on either . . . or . . ..

Complex answer to complex request

Simple requests require only normal politeness, and sometimes an appeal, to induce the reader to take the appropriate action, but in complex letters it is necessary to motivate, to persuade; this not always straightforward. Sometimes the writer has to motivate by rational argument. Sometimes it is necessary to persuade the reader to accept the facts that are unexpected and unwelcome. Moreover when you write you have not only to induce the reader to do something disagreeable but to continue to think well of you and your organisation. The points might be:

- Thanks
- Sympathise with problem
- Restate salient facts
- Indicate difficulties with proposed solution
- Suggest another course of action
- Indicate willingness to discuss further

Letters of complaint

Motivation is again important and difficult. If you are complaining, you have to persuade your correspondent to accept the complaint, and if you are answering a complaint, you may have to deal with anger. If you are replying to a justified complaint, you have to protect the rightful interests and reputation of your organisation; if you are replying to an unjustified complaint, you have to make the injustice understood and accepted, again protecting the interests of your organisation.

When the substance of a letter is likely to be disagreeable, it is good to open with a suitable expression of sympathy, or an acceptance of non-controversial facts. Always thank the complainers, for two reasons: first, it reduces the emotional temperature; second, you should be genuinely grateful for this kind of feedback. If the complaint is in any way justified, it enables you to improve the efficiency of the service you offer. If it is unjustified, it gives you the opportunity, which would not otherwise have occurred, to correct the misapprehensions and allegations of your correspondent, and prevent them giving you a bad name.

Complaining

- Facts: what happened, where, and when.
- Appeal: give the consequences of those events to you.
- Action: what you suggest they should do about it.

Rejecting a complaint

- Thank for letter, and show sympathy.
- Agree facts as far as possible
- State what facts are questioned.
- State that you are rejecting the complaint.
- Give any more explanation of rejection.
- Suggest what they should do if still troubled.

Accepting a complaint

- Thanks; brief apology.
- Agree facts in outline.
- Say what statements of theirs are unacceptable (if any).
- Say what you will do about their problem.
- Say what you will do to prevent recurrence.
- Motivate to restore confidence in the organisation; for instance by showing that the difficulty is rare.
- Motivate to restore good will by personal comments; for instance, sorry that it happened to *them*.

A letter analysed

1. Traditional punctuation and layout[1]

RICHARDS, PRICE & GREGORY
Market Square, Wellingford, Warwickshire
Tel: Wellingford 7625 ext.99[2]

23rd April, 1990[4]

A.D. Mainprice, Esq.,
Gusset and Mainprice,
Cork Street,
London W1A 4BP.[3]

Dear Mr Mainprice,[5]

Accounts for year ended 31st March, 1990[6]

I am writing to confirm[7] yesterday's[8] telephone arrangements to meet at your office on Wednesday, 30th April at 2.45 p.m. to discuss these accounts.

In particular I hope it will be possible to meet the senior staff concerned with the points relating to cost allocation mentioned in my letter of 16th April.[9]

Yours sincerely,[10]

PG/JBB[12] (J.B. Boles)[11]

2. Open punctuation and block layout[1]

RICHARDS, PRICE & GREGORY
Market Square Wellingford Warwickshire
Tel: Wellingford 7625 ext 99[2]

23 April 1990[4]

A D Mainprice Esq
Gusset and Mainprice
Cork Street
London W1A 4BP[3]

Dear Mr Mainprice

<u>Accounts for year ended 31 March 1990[6]</u>

I am writing to confirm[7] yesterday's[8] telephone arrangements to meet at your office on Wednesday 30 April at 2.45 pm to discuss these accounts.

In particular I hope it will be possible to meet the senior staff concerned with the points relating to cost allocation mentioned in my letter of 16 April.[9]

Yours sincerely[10]

(J B Boles)[11] PG/JBB[12]

Comments

1. Here are two ways of setting out a letter. The block layout and reduced punctuation is likely to be easier to type, even in the age of word processors when there are short cuts to nearly everything. Both methods, and many variants, are widely acceptable.

2. It saves time and tempers in large organisations if the letter gives the writer's extension number as well as the main telephone number.

3. It is customary to put the reader's name and address on business letters, partly to make it easier for the typist to put

the letter in the right envelope; partly so that the reader's organisation can open the letter in the post room, throw away the envelope, and send the letter by itself to the person addressed or a substitute; and partly so that the writer's carbon copy will contain a copy of the reader's name and address.

If preferred, the reader's name and address may be at the bottom of the letter, below the signature.

There is a convention in certain circles in Britain (but not in the USA), especially among the professions, to replace 'Mr' before a man's name with 'Esq.' (short for Esquire) after it, thus: A.B. Jones, Esq., M.A., ACA instead of Mr A.B. Jones, M.A., ACA. 'Esquire' is never used in full. In general correspondence 'Esq.' seems to be losing popularity, like the designation 'Gentleman' as an alternative to occupation with which it largely corresponds. However, it is associated with officers in the services, social standing, and wealth, and many readers will prefer or even expect it. As always, try to discover your reader's preference. Next, follow the conventions of your firm or business. But if you are still uncertain, 'Esq.' is the safer form to use. Do not use 'Esq.' for foreigners, as it is more courteous to use their own style of address, or for writing abroad, even to Britons, as the foreign postal service may imagine 'Esq.' is a surname.

4. Date your own letters and memoranda and indeed every written message. It is best to put the name of the month in full, or in abbreviation, but not in numerals because 1.2.90 means the 1st of February 1990 in Britain, but 2nd of January 1990 in the USA. If you give the month in full, it does not matter whether the day comes before or after the month; but 1st February 1990 seems more logical than February 1st 1990.

5. It should be part of the courtesy of a letter to address the reader by name if possible; that is, if you know the name. You do not need to know your reader well. If you cannot find out a name, the conventional alternatives are 'Dear Sir', 'Dear Madam', or 'Dear Sir or Madam'. If you address a firm or other group, you can begin 'Gentlemen' or 'Ladies' or 'Ladies and Gentlemen' without 'Dear'; or in particular letters, 'Dear Shareholders' etc. as required. But most people still use 'Dear Sirs', even though this has the false implication that all significant employees will be men, not women. There is no exact feminine equivalent of 'Dear Sirs'.

6. All letters and memoranda need a heading if they are to be

businesslike, for the same reason that reports have headings. Memoranda, and to a lesser extent letters, can have sub-headings too. Headings help to file and retrieve a letter, and it is courteous to use the same heading as the letter to which you are replying. The heading helps the reader to focus quickly on the subject; to select other documents needed to read the letter (and for this reason a heading can include reference numbers, invoice numbers, order numbers, and the like); and it may save words in the body of the letter. As with report headings, it should be concise. Put in no useless words. Do not use 're' as part of a heading: see Appendix 8; and 'Report on' is a waste too.

7. If the purpose is not explicit in the heading, make it clear at the beginning of the letter.

8. In replying to letters or memoranda, give the date of the document you are replying to. Do not use the commercialese 'inst.', 'ult.', 'prox.', or 'idem'. Usually give the date in full (see Appendix 8).

9. Paragraph your letter carefully, both to look attractive and to help the reader follow the sense. For purposes of being visually attractive, a one-page letter can afford a longer paragraph than a letter where the reader cannot see the end. A paragraph of ten lines, if it is logically defensible, can be written without disheartening the reader too much if the signature is in sight. But usually the paragraphs of a letter are shorter than in a report because the message is simpler.

10. The conventional ending if the letter begins 'Dear' and a name is 'Yours sincerely'. If the letter begins 'Dear Sir' or the nameless alternatives, it should end 'Yours faithfully'. A few organisations use 'Yours truly' as a substitute for 'Yours faithfully'.

11. Both a signature and a typed name are necessary, and usually it is convenient to give the job title of the signer with the typed name, unless it is elsewhere on the letter. The function of this is to enable the reader to know how to reply and address the writer, so any designations (Dr, Mrs, Miss, Ms, or other preference) should be added.

A letter written by one person may have to be signed by another. The signer should not imitate the writer's signature. The best layout is:

Yours sincerely (or faithfully)
The signer's signature
The signer's name typed; then 'for'; then the writer's name typed. Do not use 'per pro' unless it is legally required.

12. Most organisations have a reference code on each letter. The commonest, like this one, consists simply of the initials of the typist and the writer. It is for the convenience of the writer's organisation, and if it is at the bottom of the sheet or the end of the letter, the reply need not quote it.

If a firm needs to have the reference quoted in the reply, it should either be part of the heading, as with an invoice number, or be given at the top of the letter prefaced by the words 'Please quote in reply'. Most business stationery has printed at the top 'Our ref:' and 'Your ref:', and it is not clear whether the responder is expected to quote them in reply or not. Doubtless this means that many references are quoted when there is no need, and some are omitted when necessary.

A memorandum analysed

Gusset & Mainprice Limited MEMORANDUM[1]

To: Mr J.D. Caine, Room MB 109;
Mr S.A. Ebernezer, Room MB 207[2]

From: P.P. Flapton, Chief Accountant Room GB 53[3]
ext. 353

Date: 23rd April, 1990

Subject: FILMS: COST CENTRES

As costs of producing films have increased fourfold in the last year, the Board has decided (minute 41/90) for the year ended 31st March 1990, and for later years, to divide these costs into cost centres as follows. I have allocated cost codes.

Cost code	To include
FCC/1	Capital equipment
FCC/4	Subcontracts
FCC/3	Filming and editing
FCC/4	Scenery, props, and costume

FCC/5	Sound and recording
FCC/6	Licences and insurance
FCC/7	Other costs

Please let me know as soon as you can, and before 1st May at all events, whether you are likely to meet any 'demarcation' problems.

I should like to have by 1st May an indication of the costs in each category for each of the last three films.

cc. Mr A.B. Cooper, Room GB 30[4] 5

Comments

1. Many organisations pre-print the word 'Memorandum' at the head of the relevant stationery. It can help with the filing; the reader presumably can see that it is a memorandum without the word. The words 'To', 'From', 'Date' and 'Subject' remind the writer of the essential top data.

2. A memorandum can be addressed to two people, and should be so addressed if it calls for action from both. The postman needs enough information here, as well as on the envelope if there is one, to deliver the memorandum, but this can be quite brief.

3. Give the reader enough information to reply by writing or telephoning or calling. It can be dangerous to assume that the reader already knows.

4. Carbon copies can save time later, when it is useful to know how much information others have received.

5. This memorandum is not signed; the name is at the top. But there is some value in having a signature at the bottom, as evidence that the writer has seen it and approved it before it went out but after it was typed.

Chapter 8

Paperwork for Meetings

Kinds of meeting

Working meetings, like working documents, are never ends in themselves. They happen in order to help some other work go forward smoothly. And if the meeting is to be effective, it almost certainly requires some form of paperwork to accompany it, to set out the items for discussion at the meeting, and to record what happened and particularly what decisions were reached.

The effectiveness of the paperwork is related to the purpose of the meeting, as the effectiveness of a report depends on understanding the terms of reference; and different kinds of meeting have different kinds of paperwork. The four main kinds of working meeting are given in the table below, and discussed in the paragraphs that follow:

Meeting	*Decision taken*	*An example*
Command	by leader	Briefing meeting
Advisory	by outside body	Royal Commission
Democratic	collectively	Board of Directors
Information	none, or individually	Area Managers

Command

If the decision is taken by one person at the meeting, after listening to the advice of those present, it can be called a command meeting. It is commonly the kind of meeting between any team and their leader. A good example in industry is a briefing meeting when the manager wants to tell the working group what their objectives are, formulate a plan in their presence to meet these objectives, hear their suggestions, and then give any orders.

The manager is the only one authorised to take the decisions and the only person responsible for them, and uses the meeting to improve the decision (with the comments of those present) and to improve the implementation (because those implementing it will understand the reasons better). The supporting papers and record of the meeting, if any, will be such as the manager approves and as serve management's purposes; their form will vary widely from manager to manager and from meeting to meeting.

Advisory

An advisory meeting is one intended, like a command meeting, to help reach decisions, but where the person or body responsible for taking the decision is outside the meeting. This is the nature of a Royal Commission, where the final decision is the responsibility of the Cabinet or the legislature. Individuals are chosen for their experience, to gather and weigh evidence, and to submit collective advice to those who need it.

They will try to argue their way to a common recommendation, based on a consensus, but if after discussion they do not agree, those with different views from the majority present their views independently in a 'minority report' and these majority and minority reports give reasons as well as recommendations.

Democratic

In a democratic meeting, the meeting itself has the power, as laid down in a constitution, to take decisions, and order others to carry out the decisions. Examples of democratic meetings include the House of Commons in session, the committee meeting of a social club, and the meeting of the board of directors of a limited company. In practice there are differences, because the House of Commons normally decides matters by voting, but club committees normally decide by reaching a consensus. But all, in the last resort, decide by voting, and all owe their place at the meeting to a process of election.

The supporting paperwork has not only to help the meeting to run smoothly, to help reach decisions, and record the decisions taken and the reasons for them, but also may be needed to show the electorate what their various elected representatives are doing. There is one official record of such a meeting, often called 'minutes', whose form may be determined by the constitution that governs the meetings themselves. Decisions of democratic meetings are embodied in these minutes in a ritual way, beginning

'Resolved . . .'
or 'The Committee resolved that . . .'

or 'It was agreed that . . .'
or some similar formula.

It is the responsibility of the Secretary to write and circulate the minutes between meetings, usually after consulting the Chair. At the next meeting the minutes are amended, if necessary, and then approved by those present, and signed by the Chair, after which they have legal force as evidence of what took place.

The supporting papers for a democratic committee, particularly the minutes, allow much less freedom for the writer than the record of any other meeting, and the conventional structure is more rigid. An example of an agenda is shown in Appendix 5 and of minutes in Appendix 6.

Information

There may be value in having a meeting even if the meeting itself has no authority, to help the individuals present to take decisions. The purposes of the meeting then become simply the sum of the purposes of those present. Working papers for such a meeting will not be likely to be effective unless there is in fact a common interest, as when those present are engaged in parallel jobs and the same information is likely to be useful to all. Where this common ground does exist, as with all the area sales managers from different parts of the country, or all the safety officers from different factories in the same company, the meetings can be valuable and are likely to be held at regular intervals.

Mixed

Meetings may be a mixture of two or more of the types above. Sometimes the mixture is a muddle, as when management wish to call a meeting a 'committee' with 'minutes' and the democratic paperwork, because democracy is popular, but the meeting does not in fact have any real power and is merely advisory. Sooner or later the confusion rebounds on those who created it.

But there may be real meetings where sometimes the decision is taken by the meeting by a vote, and sometimes by one person, on personal authority; and those preparing papers for such meetings would do well to sort out the various components, and distinguish between, say, individual decisions and meeting decisions in the minutes. In particular, all the meetings should have an element of pleasure, the social element; in moderation this helps the working meeting along, although in excess it will waste time.

Cost-effective meetings

If there are 10 people at a meeting, one person talking for five minutes is costing 50 working minutes. If that person can save that five minutes, or 50 working minutes, by 15 minutes' work before the meeting, it would save 35 working minutes in all. This is the economic reason for agendas, supporting papers, and minutes; and some assessment of the costs involved would be likely to lead to more effective meetings.

The agenda

The word 'agenda' comes from the Latin meaning 'things to be done', but now it has come to be accepted as an English singular noun, unlike data or memoranda which are plural, and it is quite correct to say 'agendas' and it would be affected to say 'agendum' (see Appendix 8). There is no one word for 'item of business' in common use.

The basic structure of the agenda might be as follows:

There will be a meeting of the . . . Committee at . . . p.m.
on . . . at . . .

Agenda

1. Apologies for absence.
2. Minutes of the last meeting (enclosed).
3. Matters arising from the minutes.
4. Report from the Chair (Note 1 enclosed).
5. Correspondence.
6. Secretary's report.
7. Treasurer's report (Note 2 enclosed).
8. Report by the . . . sub-committee (Note 3 enclosed).
9.
10.
11. Any other business.
12. Date of next meeting.

At a 'command' meeting, the person in the chair can lay down the agenda required, and alter it at the meeting if necessary. At other kinds of meeting, it is normally the Secretary's responsibility to set out the agenda, but it should be agreed by the Chair; once the meeting has started it can then be altered only with the meeting's consent.

Supporting papers

Supporting papers give the answers to points which may come up at the meeting, so far as these points are predictable and the answers are available. If only two or three people are interested in the answers, it is economical to prepare the answers and let the interested members read them before the meeting. But there is a balance to be reached. If all members have to spend an hour reading supporting papers, much of them of no concern to them personally, more time will be wasted than saved.

Supporting papers have to be time-savers, well signposted with headings so that members of the meeting can skip and skim through; well written, so that papers can be grasped at first reading; and where appropriate, using pictorial presentation, so that points can be quickly assimilated.

Papers sent to members of a meeting in advance not only save time, but also lead to a better meeting and better decisions. Members have longer to think about the factors affecting the decision.

Each supporting paper should refer to the item on the agenda which it supports, and the item on the agenda should refer to the numbered enclosure or supporting paper. Under the headings that describe the matter in the paper, there may be sub-headings: the following structure may be suitable:

- Historical background
- Problem
- Alternative courses open
- Conclusion
- Recommendation.

Minutes of meetings

'Minutes' is the official word for a conventional, neutral record of a meeting, written by the secretary and agreed by the person taking the Chair, and circulated to all members between meetings, or read at the next meeting. Subject to members' comment and amendment at the meeting following the one it records, the Chair will sign the minutes as correct. This is clearly different from a report of a meeting, which any individuals may write for their own purposes and in their own manner, rather than for the collective benefit of the committee or meeting.

Minutes are the counterpart of the agenda. The agenda, before the meeting, sets out what is to happen, in what order, and provides supporting documents to enable the meeting to reach decisions. The minutes, after the meeting, report the discussion (usually in brief) that took place on each item of the agenda, and in particular what decisions were reached.

The structure of the minutes should follow the agenda of the same meeting. The agenda should begin 'The Agenda of the . . .', and minutes begin 'Minutes of the . . .', each document showing the meeting concerned. For easy cross-reference from minutes to agenda and back, the numbering and headings should if possible be the same in the minutes as in the agenda of the same meeting. Some meetings find it useful to number minutes (and items of the agenda) continuously and consecutively throughout the year, so that one minute can be completely identified by a number which signifies the year and another for the minute, without specifying the number of the meeting. Furthermore, for long minutes it will often be useful to number paragraphs. Thus 90/31.2 might mean the second paragraph of the 31st minute of this committee in 1990.

If an item on the agenda is not discussed, it is helpful to put it nonetheless as a minute, to tie in with the agenda and explain the circumstances:

> 90/6 Treasurer's Report. In the absence of the Treasurer, the committee deferred discussion of this Report.

If a new item is inserted, so that the minutes' numbering differs from the agenda, the circumstances should be explained, at least in a collective or democratic committee.

The purpose of the minutes is to help ensure that the meeting's decisions are carried out, and to provide later meetings with information that may help them reach decisions on related matters more swiftly. The minutes of a democratically elected body may also serve to show constituents what elected members are doing on their behalf.

It follows that all decisions need to be recorded clearly, with the name of the person on the committee responsible for carrying out this decision. The name of the responsible person is sometimes indicated in a special column on the right of the minutes, to make an oversight less likely.

Whether the minutes should include the discussion, and the reasons for the decision, are matters for the judgement of the secretary, consulting the Chair if necessary. Later when the minutes are read, the members of the meeting can comment. A useful axiom is that unless some member of the meeting complains that the minutes are too short, they are too long. If it is important to include discussion as well as decisions, the minutes should separate them out clearly. It is often important to make a list of points raised in discussion, but unimportant and undesirable to give the names of individuals making the point.

Indirect speech

Minutes have to be written in indirect or reported speech, not in direct speech. Direct speech might be: 'You must take my word that if we do not act here and now it will be too late!' If it were necessary to put the whole of that sentence in the minutes (which is unlikely), it would be in indirect form, as follows: He said that they must take his word that if they did not act there and then it would be too late.

The following examples will show how to convert direct speech into indirect:

- All first and second person pronouns are replaced by their third person equivalents. Thus:
  I and *you* (singular) become *he* or *she* or *him* or *her*
  we and *you* (plural) become *they* or *them*
  my becomes *his* or *her*
  our becomes *their*
  yours (singular) becomes *his* or *hers*
  yours (plural) becomes *theirs*.
- Present tense becomes past, so:
  am, *is* become *was*
  are becomes *were*
  may becomes *might*
  may have becomes *might have*
  have, has become *had*.
- Past tense becomes pluperfect, so:
  have been becomes *had been*
  was, were become *had been*.
- Future becomes conditional, so:
  will becomes *would*
  shall becomes *should*
  will have becomes *would have*.
- Time and place become more remote, for instance:
  now becomes *then*

yesterday becomes *the previous day*
today becomes *that day*
tomorrow becomes *the next day*
this becomes *that*
here becomes *there.*

Since indirect speech uses only third person pronouns, it may sometimes be necessary to give a name to show which 'she' or 'he' is meant. The Chair may say: 'Mr Fitch sends his apologies. I think he will be able to attend the next meeting.' In indirect speech this would be: 'The Chair said that Mr Fitch sent his apologies: he thought he (Mr Fitch) would be able to attend the next meeting.'

Paperwork for one-off meetings

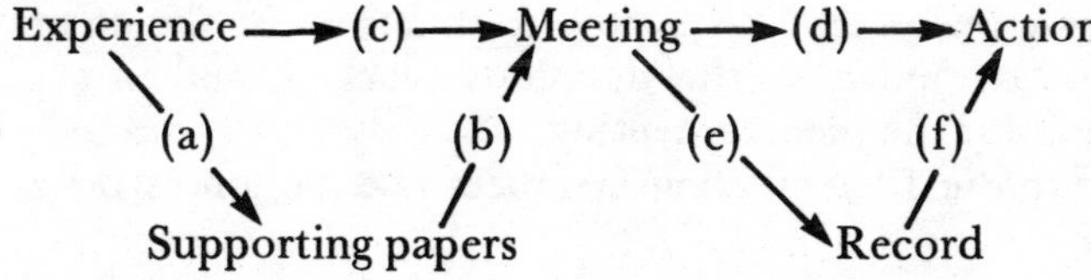

(a) The Secretary (or others concerned) collects information in writing so that those coming to the meeting can be properly briefed.
(b) All the members bring the supporting papers with them, which they have read in advance so far as they need to; spares may be available at the meeting for those who have forgotten to do so; and the information can be assumed to be common knowledge when the meeting begins.
(c) Members contribute to the meeting from their experience apart from what has been outlined in the supporting papers.
(d) After the meeting, members carry out decisions that the meeting has authorised and agreed, so far as they can.
(e) Also after the meeting the Secretary prepares a written record of the meeting; when it was held, who came, what the problem was, why the meeting came to one conclusion rather than another, and what their decision or recommendation was. The structure of this record is likely to resemble the structure of a one-off report.
(f) Members can use the record of the meeting as a check list for their own action.

Paperwork for a regular committee

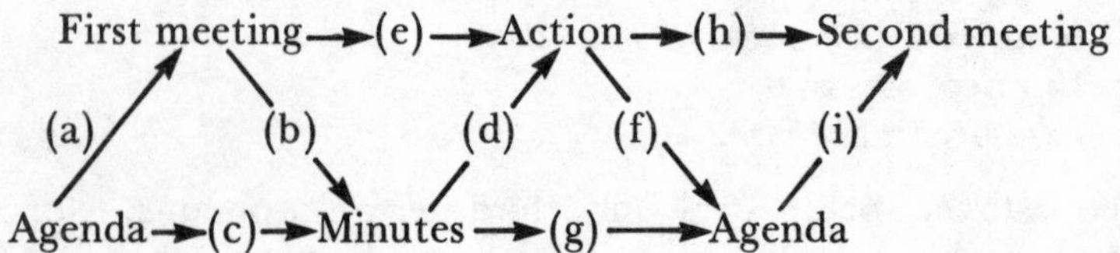

(a) The agenda determines the nature and sequence of business at the first meeting.
(b) The minutes are a record of the decisions taken at the first meeting, and of any other matters about the meeting where a permanent record is useful.
(c) The numbered minutes should refer (unless there is some reason given for doing otherwise) item by item to the numbered items of the agenda.
(d) The minutes are distributed to members of the committee, as a reminder of the decisions reached, and as a preparation for the second meeting.
(e) After the first meeting members take action as far as they can.
(f) As members take action they inform the Secretary, who uses this information in compiling the agenda and supporting papers for the second meeting.
(g) The agenda for the second meeting will include two references to the minutes of the previous meeting. One item will be 'Minutes of the last meeting', in which the minutes will be read, or if they have been distributed in advance they will be taken as read. The second meeting will have the chance to amend them if they are not right, and the agreed minutes are then signed as correct by the Chair. The next item will be 'Matters arising from the minutes' (often called simply 'Matters arising') in which any points can be dealt with which were discussed at the first meeting and have to be discussed again, unless they are important enough to have a separate item of their own.
(h) The committee meets again.
(i) Members are able to conduct business swiftly using the framework provided by the agenda and the information in the supporting papers. And so the cycle begins again.

Chapter 9

To a Wider Public

Principles

Those in business sometimes have to write documents for an increasingly wide readership, as society expects (and to some extent the law requires) commercial organisations to be accountable to interests beyond their owners and managers.

We are not talking here about advertising, which is a special art, although people who have to communicate with the public on paper should study the methods used in successful advertisements.

The groups and sectional interests to whom business is considered accountable include the local community, employees, consumers, and the nation. You may have to communicate to any of these. Clearly, executives will have to consider for each document the purposes, readers, relevance, and style of the particular document, as discussed in previous chapters. In particular the style of anything that the public will want to read and be able to follow is likely to be different from the natural writing style of a middle manager.

More firms have been providing reports for their employees at the same time as the annual Report and Accounts for shareholders. These reports we discuss in detail below. Reports for other sectional interests have not yet been produced, as far as we know; but advertisements for many large organisations have increasingly emphasised the claim of these organisations to be safeguarding the interests of these outside groups.

In writing for these groups as for any others, writers must establish the proper criteria of relevance. In particular, they must establish who their readers are, what are their preferred reading styles (see pp.17-18) and what are their expectations from reading this particular document.

The interests of readers may be of two kinds: a responsibility-interest or a worry-interest.

A responsibility-interest arises where the reader needs information to work effectively, or where information concerns the present effect of previous actions and decisions. Examples of this include:

- looking forward: information about the expected costs and returns from different investments;
- looking backward: the comparative sales figures of the same product in different areas, or different products in the same area.

Readers are not pleased by the implication that they are responsible, and if necessary to blame, for poor results, when they have no power to affect those results. It is vital, therefore, when writing a responsibility-interest report looking backwards, to distinguish between those results over which each reader has responsibility, and those outside the reader's control. Such a report should be tied in with a commitment by the manager to control and improve those results in a measurable way. Management by objectives is the systematic method of specifying the areas in which results are expected and the way in which they are to be measured, and this kind of report should be a natural part of the MBO system.

A worry-interest may be anything that affects the security of a worker's job, or any external changes that could require adaptation or training. As a basic principle, all human beings suspect change, and worry about the harm it may do to their routine, their place in the working team or in society, and their self-esteem.

Typical examples of worry-interests would include:

- anything affecting the security of the job, such as the success of the whole organisation;
- anything which could change their day-to-day work, such as micro-electronic circuitry, or any other technical development;
- anything which is appearing on the horizon which might later affect the job, such as markets in which the product was sold and in which the organisation was competing; or wider economic and political factors such as inflation.

The worry-interest has its positive side. Workers should know about the successes of the whole organisation, or any part of it that they can identify themselves with. Perhaps we should describe this as a 'pride-interest'.

In either a pride-interest or a worry-interest the reader has no control over the events, at least not a large control or a direct control. Unlike the responsibility-interest, the justification for passing on this information is not that it has an obvious effect, as an incentive, to improve performance. Sometimes the trade union may be able to insist on this kind of information as part of its access to information affecting collective bargaining; sometimes it is put out by management as a justification of some management policy. More usually, it is enough to notice that a sense of pride is likely to improve a person's job satisfaction and anxiety is likely to worsen it.

Words

Specialists who normally write to other specialists, or to readers who may be expected to know the meanings of terms they use, will have to adapt their style and language for the wider disclosure. Employee annual reports, for instance, do normally translate their accounting terms into words of one or two syllables and sentences with simple words. 'Assets', for example, become 'What we own', and 'Liabilities' become 'What we owe'. Similar translations are needed for many terms. Not only words, but the ideas they stand for and relationships between them can be confusing to the non-technical reader.

In making things simpler there is a danger of misleading the readers. For instance, to include 'depreciation' under the heading 'cash generated' in the simplified 'Source and Application of Funds Statement', contained in one employee report, confused uninitiated readers who could not understand how depreciation could lead to more cash coming in. Again, one technical word will normally have to be replaced by several short words, so that although the result is simpler it is longer. This may put off some readers. So it may be necessary to use both the technical term and the definition; although this makes the document even longer, it avoids error, and may help to educate the audience, so making it possible for understanding to be greater in the future.

Sentences and paragraphs

Chapter 3 refers to the different requirements of the educated specialist and the general public in style. The wider public prefer shorter sentences and paragraphs than professional readership. You can get some idea of the difference between educated readers and the wider public by comparing different newspapers (see pp.29-30). You may know that other executives read newspapers with large pages and small circulations, but to write effectively to the public it is essential to study the work of successful journalists on newspapers or publications with massive circulations.

Large amounts of money

The untrained mind cannot grasp the millions of pounds, or any other unusually large quantity, that the normal company report deals with. The heading '£000' may be confusing. It is often convenient to break down the amounts into more manageable units. The imagination can more readily grasp amounts with which it is accustomed to deal; which is why so many employee reports break down amounts so that the whole sum, be it sales, or value added, or profit, is £1, and the items making up that £1 are expressed as pence, giving in fact a percentage of the total. Another way may be to break up the grand total by expressing it as an amount per customer, per employee, per shareholder, per inhabitant of the United Kingdom, or per day. This may not only reduce vast amounts to a more comprehensible size, but also provide a ratio that is interesting in itself.

Pictorial presentation

Say it in pictures
You do not need to have the faintest idea how the mind works to know that one picture is worth much more than a thousand words. Anyone who goes into a bookshop can see what value publishers put on colour and pictures. If you pick up a new book which has illustrations, the odds are that you look at the illustrations first. They give you most information, in a form that you can analyse and absorb most quickly. Not only that, but it is easier to remember pictures, and the information they contain, when words and numbers have faded away.

Computer graphics
Until recently if you wanted pictures in your report or letter, even if you wanted a simple graph, it was impossible unless you had a special art department to provide it, and then expensive. The 'desktop publishing' revolution, and the development of computer graphics and laser printers, have brought the cost

down to within the range of most organisations. It is now simply whether you have the will, not the money.

There are many unexploited opportunities here. We can only deal with the more obvious ways of presenting numerical information in pictures or diagrams.

Diagram

There are many kinds, for instance family trees, organisation charts, flow process charts. Maps are a kind of diagram. They all illustrate the value of readers seeing how people, places or activities relate together.

Graph

See figure 1, below. Graphs are familiar features of newspapers. This one shows two quantities, production and employees, over six years, and also the ratio production per employee. To put such differing units on the same graph requires either two scales, usually given on either side of the graph, or another method. This graph gives each quantity as a percentage of what it was in a given year called the 'base' year.

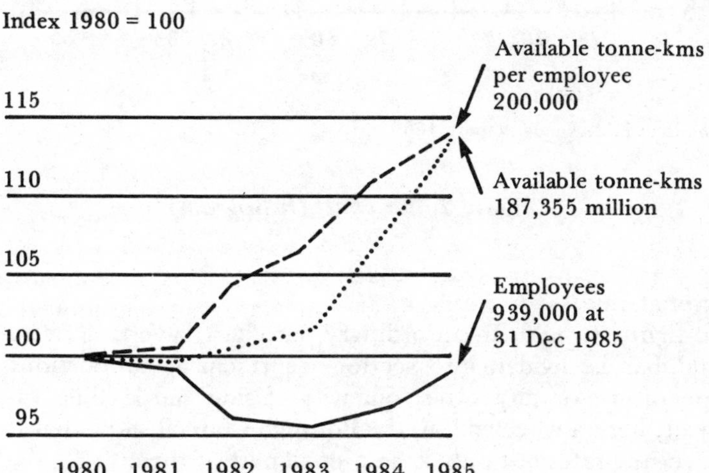

Source: IATA Management Information Division, Annual Report 1986

Figure 1. *Graph: Employees and Production 1980-1985 System – All Services*

Histogram

This is really a series of bar charts placed beside each other for comparison; see figure 2, below. This is a simple one; it would be possible to divide up each bar to show different things, say categories of membership. Then the reader could see the trend of each category over the period. It would, however, become rather congested and so difficult to read. The three-dimensional effect is easily obtained with computer graphics.

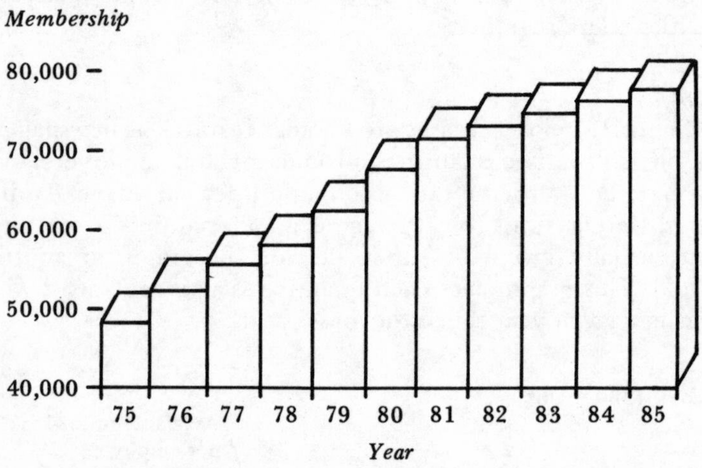

Source: BIM, Annual Report, 1985

Figure 2. *Bar chart (histogram)*

Pictobar chart

See figure 3, p.93. In an ordinary bar chart, a vertical or horizontal bar is divided into sections representing proportions of expenditure or any other quantity. Using the outline of an object, here a wheeled bin, the Borough Council show that they collect the rates but only keep a small part of them.

Pie chart

See figure 4, p.93. This kind of drawing is called a pie chart because it resembles a fruit pie cut into slices. It can analyse expenditure and income well, as here, but for those who want to know the actual amounts, they are listed too. There are no

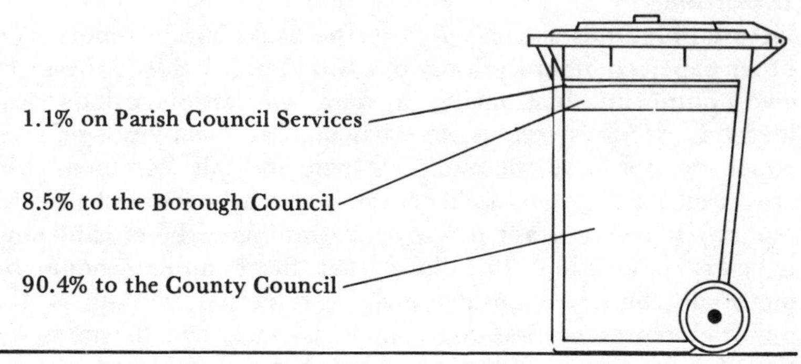

Source: Royal Borough of Windsor and Maidenhead *The Way Ahead*, 1986

Figure 3. *Pictobar chart*

percentages given, but readers can either judge for themselves roughly from the pie, or work them out accurately from the amounts given.

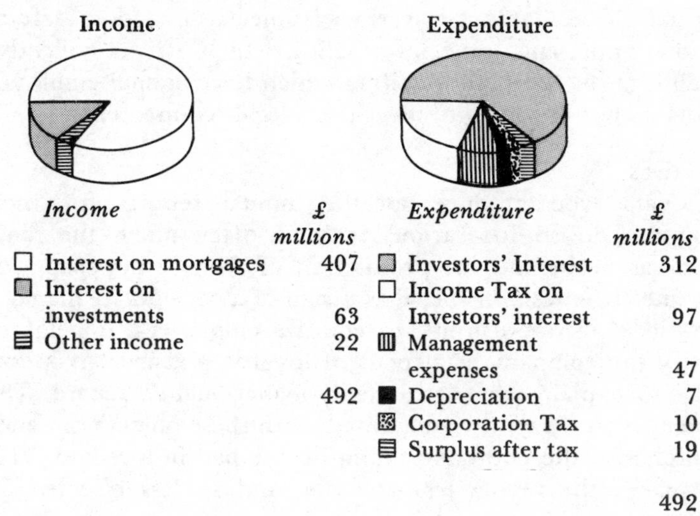

Source: Anglia Building Society, Report of Accounts 1985

Figure 4. *Pie chart*

Distortion

Pictorial methods are now rightly the backbone of reports and other paper communications to a wide public. But it is easy to give, quite unintentionally, a false impression using these methods. (This is serious, in particular, for employee reports, which do not have the auditor's 'true and fair' comment, and are circulated to an audience which may well distrust the report.) It is important for any illustrations to be credible and to carry conviction. It follows that the compiler should be pictorially honest. Consider giving the actual amount by the pictorial representation of it; and in charts and diagrams see that the pictures are in proportion so that they look right.

Employee reports

Statutory background

At present there is no statutory obligation on a firm to provide special annual reports for their employees, and many do not. The Industrial Relations Code of Practice indeed recommends it, but that Code is not legally binding. There is legislation, and more will doubtless follow, which obliges employers to make information available on various subjects, including safety, pension funds, and some information which affects collective bargaining. But even those firms which have annual employee reports do not use them to meet these legal requirements.

Objectives

Employers who produce specific annual reports for their employees do so for various reasons; often much the same reasons as lie behind the production of a house newspaper or magazine. It is fashionable, it is a sign of a considerate management, it is an opportunity to educate employees, it helps to identify the company as a focus of loyalty, and it is an opportunity to explain (that is, defend) management's record. The problem is that a report, unaudited, with these objectives, tends to emphasise the good and minimise the bad in a record. This bias makes the report less credible, and so less effective in achieving its objectives. Some companies maximise profits in the shareholders' report, by ignoring inflation, while explaining inflation carefully in the employees' report to show how little real profits have grown. This kind of cheating must undermine confidence.

It might be the answer in the long run to arrange for the

employee reports to be audited in some way acceptable to the employees, to provide a guarantee of some objectivity in the report, and to bring the responsibility of the management to the employees on to the same basis as the responsibility to shareholders.

It is now established that employees are interested more in what concerns their own unit than in the whole organisation. 'Units' may be of many sizes; it seems likely that the larger the unit the less interest any one employee will feel in how it is doing. A single person cannot much influence the results. Employee reports can never wholly answer this difficulty; briefing groups, described in the next section, are essential for that. However, some companies give an account of the performance during the year of each of the main parts or segments of the whole organisation; and others have a pull-out supplement for each segment, giving the annual results for that segment, which is then distributed only to the employees in the segment concerned.

Briefing groups: writing the brief

Management frequently passes information to employees at meetings of small groups, or teams, addressed by the manager or supervisor in charge of the group. Such meetings are called briefing meetings or briefing groups, and if the manager or supervisor has a written sheet containing notes for the meeting, the sheet may be called the 'brief'. The brief may contain information pertinent to the group concerned, such as the cost of raw materials used, the value of the products generated, or forecasts and targets for the future.

The advantage of briefing groups compared to the annual employee report is that there is face-to-face communication: the supervisor or manager can explain the brief in terms suitable for the particular audience, can invite questions, and answer them; can sense the worries of the group and prepare to meet their problems in advance; and can more effectively co-ordinate and motivate the group.

The manager preparing the brief should discuss it with the manager or supervisor who is to use it. It may be important for several briefing groups to hear the same news the same way. There may be categories of information: that which the supervisor needs to know but is not to be passed on; that which it is essential to pass on; and information which may be useful for question time, or where the supervisor has to decide whether to pass it on or not. The brief should make it clear where these distinctions are drawn.

Sometimes it may be essential to pass on information to the members of the group in written or pictorial form, using a sheet for distribution, an overhead projector, or a poster. A distributed sheet is more suitable where the exact wording of the message is important, or where the groups need to give the matter some thought; it is obviously less suitable for confidential matters, or with unsophisticated audiences.

The value of the briefing groups for making more realistic contact with employers than through employee reports, is shown in the story told in the Touche Ross report *Employees and the Employee Report.*

> A middle-aged woman clerk in a factory, on her first day of employment with the company, had been shown into a small office and her task of processing invoices explained. She had then carried out this job for the next five years with very little contact with anyone else except for the clerks who brought and took away her work. One day, without explanation, she received upon her desk an Employee Report stating that the company had made a profit of £X million. There were a large number of colourful bar charts showing where the money came from and where it went. When I interviewed her and mentioned involvement, she pointed out that in five years no one had ever shown her over the factory, she was even uncertain as to the products of the company, she had never seen and would not recognise the factory general manager and, finally, £X million was beyond any experience she had of money.

Appendices

Appendix 1

Specimen Terms of Reference

REPORT OF THE COMPANY LAW COMMITTEE

To The Rt. Hon. Frederick Erroll, M.P.,
President of the Board of Trade.

1. We were appointed by your predecessor on the 10th December, 1959 "To review and report upon the provisions and working of the Companies Act, 1948, the Prevention of Fraud (Investments) Act, 1958, except in so far as it relates to industrial and provident societies and building societies, and the Registration of Business Names Act, 1916, as amended; to consider in the light of modern conditions and practices, including the practice of takeover bids, what should be the duties of directors and the rights of shareholders; and generally to recommend what changes in the law are desirable."

2. We now have the honour to submit our Report.

3. In response to personal invitations and advertisements in the Press we received a substantial body of written evidence bearing upon the matters under review from individuals, companies, Government departments and trade and professional organisations concerned in one capacity or another with the operation of this branch of the law: in all more than 300 memoranda or letters were received. At our request the written evidence contributed was, to facilitate collation, for the most part arranged in accordance with headings listed in a standard form of questionnaire provided by us, which now appears in Appendix A to this Report. In many cases the written evidence submitted was supplemented by oral evidence, which, with the written evidence to which it referred, was printed and published as our enquiry proceeded (Minutes of Evidence taken before the Company Law Committee and published by Her Majesty's Stationery Office). The names of the witnesses who gave oral evidence are listed in Appendix B. The evidence both written and oral has been of the greatest possible assistance to us and we would here record our indebtedness to all those who took part in providing it. Our special thanks are due to the distinguished witnesses from the U.S.A.:–

Mr. Manuel F. Cohen, Director, Division of Corporation Finance, Securities and Exchange Commission (now a Commissioner of the Securities and Exchange Commission),

Professor Louis Loss, Law School, Harvard University,

Mr. Henry S. Morgan, Mr. John M. Young and Mr. Frank A. Petito, of Morgan Stanley & Co., New York,

Mr. George A. Brownell and Mr. Frederick A.O. Schwarz, of Davis Polk Wardwell Sunderland and Kiendl, New York.

Mr. C.D. McDaniel of Arthur Andersen & Co.,

for coming here to give evidence and for the remarkably lucid and interesting account they gave us of American law and practice.

Appendix 2

Examples of Numbering

2.1 Civil Service

any document "required by or for the purposes of any of the provisions of this Act specified in the Fifteenth Schedule hereto." We cannot see why the offence should be limited to documents etc. required by or for the purposes of the provisions specified in the Fifteenth Schedule and we think that it should extend to documents required for any of the purposes of the Act.

511. **We recommend that:**

(a) **section 428 should be extended to cover defaults by officers of the company and to cover defaults either by the company or by its officers in complying with any of their statutory duties;**

(b) **the Court should be empowered on the application of the Registrar of Companies to order a company which is in persistent breach of its statutory duties to be wound up; and in particular this general power should be exercisable if, after the lapse of a prescribed period, the company has failed to appoint a secretary or the statutory minimum of directors or has failed to pay the annual registration fee which we have recommended elsewhere;**

(c) **the Court should be empowered on the application of the Registrar of Companies to order a company to be wound up if it is satisfied that the company is being carried on for an unlawful purpose (including a purpose lawful in itself but one which cannot lawfully be carried out by a registered company);**

(d) **the Court should be empowered on the application of the Registrar of Companies to order a company to be struck off the register and dissolved without winding up, if in the circumstances, winding up would not be appropriate;**

(e) **the reference in section 438 to the Fifteenth Schedule should be repealed.**

Foreign Companies and Other Matters

Foreign companies

512. The provisions of Part X of the Act apply to companies incorporated outside Great Britain. Sections 406-416 apply to such companies if they establish a place of business in Great Britain, when they are described as "overseas companies". Sections 417-423 apply to the issue in

Great Britain of prospectuses and offers for sale relating to shares or debentures of companies incorporated outside Great Britain and apply whether the companies concerned have established a place of business in Great Britain or not.

513. Oversea companies must furnish the Registrar of Companies with copies of their constitutions, particulars of their directors and secretary and the name and address of at least one person resident in Great Britain authorised to accept on behalf of the company service of process and

2.2 Alpha-numeric

4. Presentation

(a) Style

Remember that you are writing a document with a strictly limited objective. It is not meant to entertain, inspire or exhort. *Its sole purpose is to provide a factual record of the meeting.*

It follows that your sentences should be short; your words simple; your expression direct and to the point; and your meaning clear and capable of only one interpretation. The English language is a precision tool. Use it like a craftsman. The result will be elegant in its simplicity and efficient in the performance of its task.

(b) Names

The attribution of views to individuals in the Minutes is, on balance, undesirable. The inclusion of names tends to lengthen the Minutes without adding to their usefulness. It also provides potential grounds for complaint by individuals who may feel that their views have not been adequately reported, or that their names appear less frequently than they consider justified by the number of their interventions.

Exceptions to this practice, such as reports and special contributions by individuals, will readily come to mind.

(c) Layout

(i) Attendance Record. Two methods of recording attendance can be recommended. The first is in common use: Names are simply listed under 'Present' and 'Apologies for Absence.' The drawback of this method is that it makes no provision for those members who were absent but did not send apologies; neither does it give a bird's eye view of the attendance record as a whole.

These objections are overcome in the second method. All members are listed, but those present are distinguished by some typographical device, such as printing their names in capital letters. If desired, a further sign can be added to indicate those of the absent members who sent apologies.

(ii) Numbering. Each Minute should be numbered consecutively from the first meeting onwards. In some cases it may be more convenient to begin each set of Minutes, or each year, with '1'. Whatever method is employed, the number should always be used when referring to a Committee Minute. (See also para 5 (b)(ii), p. 9).

2.3 Decimal

3.6 *Introduction, Main Text, Conclusions and Recommendations*

3.6.1 *Introduction* The introduction should briefly show the origin, scope and objects of the work, how it fits in with past work and how the work has been tackled.

3.6.2 *Main Text* The main text shall be divided into numbered sections, sub-sections being indicated by the use of a decimal point. Descriptions of test apparatus, test methods, measured results and discussion of results shall be in separate sections. References shall be collected together into a separate section at the end of the report, and shall be indicated in the text by the number of the reference in Arabic numerals as a superscript without brackets at the appropriate place in the text. Small tables can be incorporated in the main text. Large tables are best collected into a separate section at the end of the report. Symbols should conform to standard usage, eg BS 1991[2] and a separate list of symbols should be provided. Equations shall be numbered consecutively throughout the paper. All pages shall be numbered, the numbers to run consecutively throughout the paper. The security grading of reports graded confidential and above shall appear on each page. All measurements should desirably be reported in SI units (see BS 3763:1970)[4].

3.6.3 *Conclusions* The conclusions reached in the report should normally appear as a self-contained section at the end of the main text. New facts shall not be introduced.

3.6.4 *Recommendations* If recommendations for further action are made, these shall be given separately from "conclusions".

3.7 *Acknowledgements*

3.7.1 Acknowledgements of help given in preparing the paper or supplying information shall be made in a separate section.

3.8 *List of References*

3.8.1 References shall be listed in the order in which they appear in the text. The order within each item shall be author's name (surname first, title of the report or journal article referred to, report reference, or journal title abbreviated according to an accepted system, eg BS 4148[3]. Volume numbers shall be underlined, and inclusive page numbers given not preceded by "pages" or "pp". Dates of all references shall be given, when known, in brackets at the end of the reference.

3.8.2 Reports of a higher security grading than that of the paper being written shall be listed by author's name, report number and date only.

3.9 *Definitions*

3.9.1 Where unusual terms are employed, or well-known terms used in a restricted sense, definitions of these terms shall be presented in a separate section, a reference to this section being given in the main text when the term is first introduced.

3.10 *Tables*

3.10.1 Extensive tables shall be grouped together in a separate section in the order in which they are mentioned in the main text, the pages being numbered consecutively with the preceding matter. Tables shall be identified by Arabic numerals, and their titles and column headings shall be self-explanatory.

Appendix 3

Specialised Documents

3.1 Post-audit management letters

Name & Address of Client **Date**

Dear Sir,

Internal Control

In the course of our interim audit for the year ended 31st December 19.., we examined the principal internal controls which your company has established to ensure, as far as possible, the accuracy and reliability of its accounting records, and to safeguard its assets. As we agreed at our meeting of . . . we are now writing to inform you of the weaknesses in control revealed by our audit examination and to suggest improvements to overcome those weaknesses.

As we also explained at our meeting, our examination was undertaken solely to enable us to express an audit opinion. Accordingly we have not undertaken an exhaustive investigation of every possible weakness, and this letter should not be regarded as constituting an exhaustive list of all the shortcomings in the systems.

(The detailed comments would now follow. An illustrative extract is included covering Purchases. The structure of each point is noted on the right.)

4. PURCHASES

4.1 *Authorisation of Orders*	*Summary of weakness*
The Company recognises the importance of strict control over the raising of orders and for this reason has established a centralised Buying Department and requires the Chief Buyer to authorise each order before it is placed.	*Company procedure*
Our tests indicated that in x out of a zample of y orders the Chief Buyer had authorised the requisition and not the order, while in a further z cases there had been no authorisation at all.	*Circumstances of weakness*
The reason we were given for this was that buying department staff were under great pressure of work and the Chief Buyer was not always available.	*Cause of weakness*
While our tests did not reveal any cases of improper orders, it would appear that the system would not detect these if they occurred. This could result in substantial loss to the Company.	*Possible effect of weakness*

We recommend that the Chief Buyer keeps a record of all invoices he has authorised and checks periodically to ensure that the numeric sequence is complete. He can easily achieve this by filing his copy numerically. Any missing documents should be thoroughly investigated and explained. *Recommendation*

We understand that the Chief Buyer accepts this recommendation and intends to use his secretary to ensure that order number sequences are all accounted for. *Acceptability of recommendations to staff involved*

4.2 *Quality Check of Goods Received* *Summary heading*

In order that payment for defective goods is not made the Company's accounting procedure requires that Material Control conduct a quality test and note their satisfaction, or otherwise, on the Goods Received Notes. This should be done before the distribution of Goods Received Notes. *Company procedure* In our audit testing of . . . Goods Received Notes we found that every accounts payable department copy had been detached and forwarded before Material Control had conducted their check. We understand that this occurs so as not to cause delays in the accounts department in processing deliveries and making payment, which would otherwise occur, because of the continuous backlog of work in Material Control. *Circumstances of weakness*

However, this practice makes a major systems control ineffective, and makes it likely that occasionally the Company will pay for defective goods. Our testing revealed . . . instances of this, involving goods totalling £. . . *Possible effect of weakness*

We recommend that management strengthen the staffing levels in Material Control to reduce the backlog of work. We also recommend the departments concerned to follow strictly the procedures laid down. To avoid losing discounts for prompt payment we recommend that Buying Department indicate such discounts on the Goods Inwards copy order, so that these deliveries receive priority checking and the documentation can be passed promptly to the accounts payable department. *Recommendation*

We understand that after an internal reorganisation the company is allocating another member of staff to Material Control. The Chief Buyer has also agreed that orders involving discount can be marked to ensure prompt attention. *Recommendation acceptable to staff involved*

4.3 . . . . .

Minor Internal Control Weakness

We set out in an Appendix a list of minor weaknesses to which we also wish to draw your attention.

We would appreciate your informing us of the steps you decide to take on these matters; in particular your confirmation that you have carried out the agreed changes.

Please inform us also of any changes in the existing system of internal control, as they are made.

Yours faithfully,

. . . . .

Another way of presenting detailed matter:

4. PURCHASES

4.2 *Quality Check of Goods Received*

In order that payment for defective goods is not made the Company's accounting procedure requires that Material Control conduct a quality test and note their satisfaction, or otherwise, on the Goods Received Notes. This should be done before the distribution of Goods Received Notes. In our audit testing of . . . Goods Received Notes we found that every accounts payable department copy had been detached and forwarded before Material Control had conducted their check. We understand that this occurs so as not to cause delays in the accounts department in processing deliveries and making payment, which would otherwise occur, because of the continuous backlog of work in Material Control.
However, this practice makes a major systems control ineffective and makes it likely that occasionally the Company will pay for defective goods. Our testing revealed . . . instances of this, involving goods totalling £ . . .

We recommend that management strengthen the staffing levels in Material Control to reduce the backlog of work. We also recommend the departments concerned to follow strictly the procedures laid down. To avoid losing discounts for prompt payment we recommend that Buying Department indicate such discounts on the Goods Inwards copy order, so that these deliveries receive priority checking and the documentation can be passed promptly to the accounts payable department.

We understand that after an internal reorganisation the Company is allocating another member of staff to Material Control. The Chief Buyer has also agreed that orders involving discount can be marked to ensure prompt attention.

3.2 Non-routine report

Meeting of Wibley District Health Authority X Committee, 18 September 1995: Agenda item 5.

Waiting Lists — By P Barribault, District Information Officer

1. Proposals.

   1.1 That the Information Section carry out a survey every six months to check whether the waiting lists are accurate.

1.2 That the Authority implement a district-wide Admissions policy to help those waiting a long time, such as for General Surgery at Wibley General Hospital.

1.3 That the Authority consider whether to take any other action on the waiting lists.

2. Relevant Previous Decisions.

In the July meeting of the DHA (minute 100/95) members discussed an 'Annual Report on Wibley Health Authority Activity 1994', and asked for a report on Wibley's waiting lists.

3. Reasons

3.1 Five Year Trends in Wibley DHA and the Region.

The District waiting list has risen from 3128 in March 1990 to 3766 in March 1995, partly from a drop in admissions over the period from 17,648 in 1990 to 17,206 in 1994. The continued expansion of day case activity should reduce the waiting lists. The Regional list fell slightly, from 34,743 to 34,273.

3.2 Proportion of People Waiting for More Than a Year in 1990 & 1995

This has remained the same, 36%, for General Surgery at the former Wibley Unit; rose from 1% to 3% for General Surgery at the Haddock Unit, and from 0 to 5% for Oral Surgery at the Wibley Unit. All other specialties at Wibley and Haddock, and the DHA and the Region, show a fall in this proportion over five years. However, in General Surgery in the Wibley Unit 464 people on the list in March 1995 had been waiting over a year. A district-wide Admissions policy would help to deal with this problem.

3.3 The Waiting Experience of Patients Admitted

There is wide variation between specialties and hospitals. The longest average wait was 24 weeks for oral surgery at Wibley General Hospital; the shortest 4 weeks for gynaecology at Haddock General Hospital. The average wait for General Surgery was 14 weeks at Wibley General Hospital and 8 weeks at Haddock General Hospital.

3.4 Are the Waiting Lists Genuine?

We are now making a survey to check the waiting lists. We asked urgent cases which had been waiting for over one month, and others over three months, whether they wished to remain on the waiting list. Of the 1377 letters sent out, 862 (63%) have been returned so far, and of those responses 137 (16%) did not wish to remain on the list.

Appendix 4

Example of Routine Report

Monthly Profit & Sales Figures
Feb. 1989

Confidential to Production Committee: until released.

Total Sales: £117,140

Total Profits: £7,034

	Area A £	Area B £	Area C £
Month's sales	64,374	41,291	11,475
Target sales	60,000	30,000	30,000
Variance	+ 7%	+ 38%	– 62%
Last year sales	55,703	26,814	25,305
Month's profit (loss)	4,922	5,809	(3,697)
Target profit	4,000	4,000	4,000
Variance	+ 922	+1,809	–7,697
Last year's profit (loss)	3,947	3,580	3,271

Comments: The disappointing figures from Area C are caused mainly by the industrial disputes at the works of both our major customers. Costs of stockholding until the dispute is over have increased the loss in this area for February.

The good results for Area B can be attributed largely to the fact that three customers have substantially increased their orders for this month. It is not yet clear whether this increase will be permanent.

(A.D. Scott, Assistant Accountant)

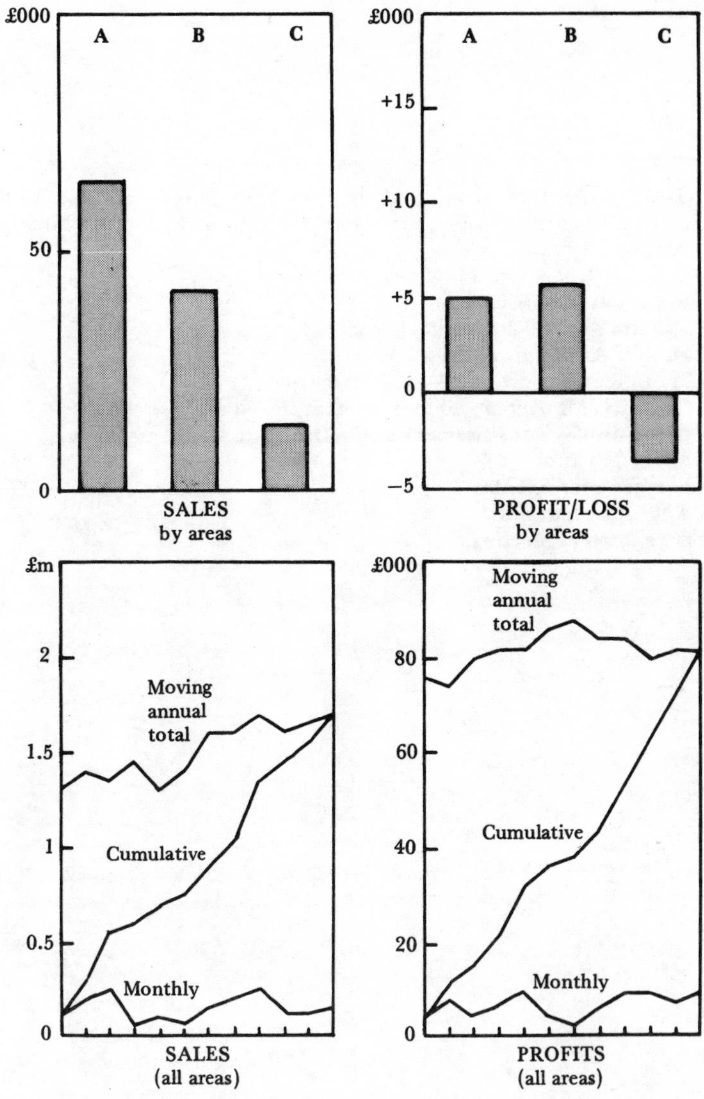
£000
A
B
C
50
0
SALES
by areas
£000
A
B
C
+15
+10
+5
0
−5
PROFIT/LOSS
by areas
£m
2
1.5
1
0.5
0
Moving
annual
total
Cumulative
Monthly
SALES
(all areas)
£000
80
60
40
20
0
Moving
annual
total
Cumulative
Monthly
PROFITS
(all areas)

Appendix 5

Specimen Agenda

AGENDA for the 10th Meeting of the Hall Extension Committee, to be held in the Committee Room, Droitgate Library, at 8 p.m. on Monday 8th November, 1999.

1. **Apologies for Absence.**
2. **Minutes of the 9th Meeting** (attached).
3. **Matters Arising from the Minutes.**
4. **Treasurer's Report** (see Note 1 attached).
5. **Publicity.** Mr. Kemp will propose that the committee should take a display advertisement in the Droitgate Courier (schedule of charges attached).
6. **Forthcoming Events.**
7. **Any Other Business.**
8. **Date of Next Meeting.**

Appendix 6

Specimen Minutes

Minutes of the 10th meeting of the Hall Extension Committee, held in the Committee Room, Droitgate Library, at 8 p.m., Monday 8th November, 1999.

Present: D.O. Allen (Chairman), D.F. Evans (Secretary), E.L. Kemp (Treasurer), P.T. Mead.

In attendance: F.A. Pope, M.L. Stubbs.

The Chairman welcomed Mr. Pope, from the District Council, and Mr. Stubbs from the Red Cross.

1. **Apologies for Absence.** M.P. Wicks, W. York.

2. **Minutes of the last meeting.** Item 4, Planning permission, after the words "the committee agreed" should be added the words "subject to approval at the A.G.M.".

With this amendment the minutes were agreed, and signed by the Chairman.

3. **Matters Arising.**

3.1 Opening Ceremony. The Secretary reported that he had received a letter from the Duke of Dunstable refusing an invitation to open the extension. — ACTION

3.2 Charity Commission. The Secretary reported that he had not yet had a reply from the Charity Commission about the proposed change in the Objectives.

4. **Treasurer's Report.**

Balance B/fwd from last report	£2,375
Income since last report	1,045
Expenditure since last report	975
Balance C/fwd	2,445
Forecast short-term income	1,800
Liabilities and foreseeable payments	1,600

5. **Publicity.** Mr. Kemp proposed that the committee should take a display advertisement in the Droitgate Courier. Points raised in discussion were:

(a) it was important to attract local interest and local funds;

(b) display advertisements of an effective size were expensive;

(c) the committee still hoped for an article on the Hall

in the near future which would be more effective than an advertisement.

The proposal was withdrawn.

6. **Forthcoming Events.**

Friday 3rd December, Wine and Cheese. DFE

Monday 27th December. Boxing Day Dance. ELK

AGREED: To organise an exhibition of the Hall's history in February. DOA

7. **Any Other Business.**

Subscriptions. The Treasurer asked for the views of members on the level of subscriptions. The committee agreed to have a full discussion at the next meeting. DFE

8. **Date of Next Meeting.** Monday 13th December, 1999, at 8 p.m., in the Committee Room of the Droitgate Library.

Appendix 7

Bibliography

Style

H.W. Fowler. *A Dictionary of Modern English Usage* (revised by Sir Ernest Gowers). Oxford University Press, 1965

H.W. Fowler and F.G. Fowler. *The King's English.* Oxford University Press, 3rd edition, 1973.

Sir Ernest Gowers. *The Complete Plain Words* (revised by Sidney Greenbaum and Janet Whitcut). Her Majesty's Stationery Office, 1986

Oxford Paperback Dictionary. Oxford University Press, 2nd edition, 1983

Roget's Thesaurus. Penguin, 1984

British Standards Institution. *The preparation of British Standards for building and civil engineering: Part 2. Guide to presentation* (PD 6501: Part 2: 1984)

Casey Miller and Kate Swift. *The Handbook of Non-sexist Writing.* The Women's Press, 1981

Plain English Campaign

Tom Vernon. *Gobbledegook.* National Consumer Council, 1980

Richard Thomas. *Plain Words for Consumers.* National Consumer Council, 1984

Structure

British Standards Institution. *Specification for the Presentation of Research and Development Reports* (BS:4811:1972)

Bruce Cooper. *Writing Technical Reports.* Penguin, 1964

Paperwork for Meetings

P.J.C. Perry. *Hours into Minutes.* BACIE, 1986

Appendix 8

Points of Style

Definitions and aims

'The authorities', in this appendix, mean *The King's English* by Fowler and Fowler; Fowler's *Modern English Usage*, revised by Gowers; and Gowers's *Complete Plain Words*, revised by Greenbaum and Whitcut. These are authorities because they are accepted as such more widely than any others; because they explain and justify their principles logically; and because they show how these principles lead to effective writing.

'The pedants', in this appendix, are those who follow certain popular superstitions about what is correct English, although these superstitions do not make writing more effective and are condemned by the authorities.

We have written this book respecting the authorities and ignoring the pedants, and recommend others to do the same where they can. But often an executive's writing is bound to be scrutinised in detail, and to be 'safe' and avoid giving offence or provoking even unjustified criticism, you may have to defer to the pedants as well as the authorities. The appendix takes this into account.

above.
The above committee . . .
The above-mentioned articles . . .
. . . for the purpose above . . .
Pedants object to this use of 'above' but the authorities defend it. It is safer, shorter, and more direct to say 'this' or 'these' instead of 'above': 'This committee', 'these articles', 'for this purpose'. If it is not clear what 'this' or 'these' refer to, 'the above' will be obscure too.

active and passive. See p.30.

adjectives and nouns. Keep adjectives close to the nouns they describe, and avoid howlers like 'Chair for sale by lady with stuffed seat', or 'The flotation from the bank, which is substantial, but subject to some government regulations, should be completed shortly.'

Does the phrase 'which is substantial' apply to the flotation or to the bank?

advise. Commercial English has long used this word to mean 'inform': 'I have to advise you that the goods have not yet been received.' The term 'Advice note' confirms this usage. But there is no reason, here or in other ways, to keep commercial English alive. Use 'advise' to mean 'give advice': 'We advise you to review the figures quarterly'. In place of 'advise that', use 'tell', 'say', 'inform', or 'announce'.

agenda. The authorities say that this word, which is Latin for 'things to do', has now been naturalised as an English singular noun. It means 'list of items for a meeting', and can therefore have an English plural 'agendas'. It would be correct to say either 'The Agenda *is* incomplete' or 'The *Agendas* have been circulated'. It is not consistent, then, to describe one item on the agenda as an 'agendum', and 'item' is the more usual word.

alternative.
We shall be forced to choose an alternative supplier.
There appear to be three alternatives.
Pedants object to the first sentence on the grounds that 'alternative' does not mean 'another', and to the second because the Latin 'alter' means one of two, not of three or more. The authorities object only to the first. To play safe, avoid both uses. In the first sentence, 'another' is shorter as well as more correct. In the second, there may be no exact one-word synonyms of the noun 'alternative', though 'choice' or 'option' will sometimes serve. If necessary use two or more words: 'other courses' or 'other plans' for instance.

and and **but** to begin a sentence. See p.27.

anticipate. The authorities are not keen on using this word to mean 'expect', and pedants object strongly. It means to use something before the proper time, or to forestall. 'To anticipate marriage' means to live as married before the ceremony; 'to anticipate income' means to spend it before it has been paid in. The meaning is worth preserving. Use 'expect' if that is what you mean.

apostrophes. An apostrophe means first that one or more letters have been left out:
Isn't = is not; it's = it is, or it has.
Normal plurals do not have apostrophes:
Employees. Stocks.
The men were grouped in 2s and 3s.
The Board included two J.P.s and three D.S.O.s (or JPs and DSOs).
The normal possessive is xxx's:
The address of the Stock Exchange = The Stock Exchange's address.
For a plural possessive, where the plural ends in s, the possessive adds an apostrophe after the s:
The report of the auditors = the auditors' report.
The strength of foreign currencies = the foreign currencies' strength.
If the plural has no final s, then the possessive adds 's to the plural:
The rights of women = women's rights.
For a name or other singular noun, the possessive usually adds 's whether the noun ends in s or not:
Mary's lamb; St. James's Park; the actress's beauty.
The only possessive pronoun that has an apostrophe is 'one's':
Mine, yours, his, hers, its, one's ours, theirs.

The boy who put the powder on the noses of the faces of the ladies of the harem of the court of King Caractacus.	=	The boy who put the powder on King Caractacus's court's harem's ladies' faces' noses.

appreciate. In the specialist sense, this is a useful word:

There is no provision for capital appreciation.

In most other senses it is unnecessary, longwinded or ambiguous:

It is appreciated = We know
It will be appreciated = You know
You will appreciate = Can't you understand?

approximately. This is not a good substitute for 'about' or 'roughly', because it is longer, and because it means 'closely', 'nearly correct'. The more approximate an estimate is, the closer it is to the truth; but few will understand it that way.

a priori. This means 'from stated assumptions'. Avoid using it.

as far as . . . is concerned. This long expression is usually unnecessary.

Expenditure is charged in the profit and loss account in the year in which it is incurred as far as research and development are concerned.

Our thoughts often come out in that roundabout way, but there is no need to write them down like that. This could be:

Expenditure on research and development is charged in the profit and loss account in the year in which it is incurred.

assist. Prefer the short, familiar, Saxon 'help'.

as to. Leave this out of such expressions as: 'as to whether', 'as to which'.
Wrong: 'We cannot make a judgement as to whether the allowance is deductible.'
Often it can be replaced by another preposition: 'of', 'in', 'about'.
Wrong: We cannot make a judgement as to the valuation of stock.'
The authorities allow 'as to' as a way of introducing something at the beginning of the sentence which would otherwise go later, but even this is not attractive:

As to fixed assets, we can make no assessment until the accounts for the subsidiaries are available.

There is no objection to the phrase 'so as to':
Right: 'Depreciation should be allocated to accounting periods so as to charge a fair proportion to each accounting period during the expected useful life of the asset.'

author. 'The authors hereby acknowledge the help of . . .' Although this usage is widespread, it makes no sense unless the person writing it is referring to some other authors. Neither this, nor the even odder 'the present author', is a logical substitute for 'I' or 'We'.

between.
Wrong: 'The choice is between a historical basis or a current purchasing power basis.'
Either omit 'between' or change 'or' to 'and'. The items after 'between' must be separated by 'and'.
Right: 'Revenue will be divided between participating employees.'
There used to be pedants who objected to dividing something between more than two; they argued that what is 'between' two people must be 'among' several. This view has been condemned by the authorities and it is now probably safe to use 'between' regardless of the number.

brackets and punctuation. If a comma, semicolon, or colon comes at the end of a bracket, it should go outside the bracket:
Wrong: Costs were reallocated (including the discount,) and . . .
Right: Costs were reallocated (including the discount), and . . .
The only time a full stop goes inside a bracket is when the whole sentence after the previous full stop is inside the bracket. One bracket can contain several sentences if necessary.

capital letters. Although in handwriting block capitals are easier to read than small letters, in print the opposite is true. A page all in capitals would be tiring to read. Motorway signs use lower case letters because then the driver can see the word and read it from its shape more easily from a distance. It is normal to use capitals for the first letter in

- a sentence,
- names of people, places, and gods,
- days (Monday) and months (January).

In the titles or headings of institutions (House of Commons), particular jobs (Head of Marketing) or particular man-made works (*Measure for Measure*) it is normal to have capitals for the first letter of the first word and the first letter of any important words following. Consistency is important; therefore an organisation that tries to present a uniform style to its clients and public should guide its writing and typing staff in the use of capitals.

case.
In the case of . . .
. . . is the case with . . .
. . . as was the case.
In many cases . . .
In these phrases the word 'case' is an abstract noun of little meaning, and the sentence can usually be improved by a rearrangement without it:

> We appreciate that in some cases, for example in that of the wholly owned subsidiary, one subscriber and member will continue to be a mere nominee, but even in the case of a wholly owned subsidiary this helps to draw attention to the fact that it is a separate corporate entity.

could be:

> We know that sometimes, for example with a wholly owned subsidiary, one subscriber and one member will continue to be a mere nominee, but this helps to emphasise that the wholly owned subsidiary is a separate corporate entity.

ceiling. In business and the professions people often need to refer to a limit or a maximum. These words 'limit' and 'maximum', are better than the metaphorical 'ceiling' (or 'floor' for minimum) which can be ludicrous. Gowers produces this example:

> In determining the floor space, a ceiling of 15,000 square feet should normally be the limit.

character. Like 'case', 'character' is an empty abstract noun, and objects 'of a . . . character' are simply . . . objects. The meaning may not be identical; there is a difference in emphasis between payments of a fraudulent character and fraudulent payments. It ought not to be difficult, with help from a Thesaurus if necessary, to find the word that fits: perhaps false, misleading, deceitful, or deceptive payments.

colloquial abbreviations. I'll, we've, didn't etc. These abbreviations can be effective between friends but are conventionally unsuitable for a document of serious tone going to many readers, or from one organisation to another.

commas as brackets. Most people handle brackets without difficulty, but are liable to slip when using commas to do the work of brackets. There must be two commas corresponding to the two brackets otherwise necessary:
Wrong: Current estimates indicate that, in the absence of unforeseen circumstances net revenue should again increase.
There should be a second comma after 'circumstances'. If the message inside the bracket is incidental to the rest of the sentence, brackets are better than commas; prefer commas if the whole sentence cannot be understood without the part bracketed off.

commas for defining clauses.

> Payments received which are not matched with invoices have been inaccurately recorded.
>
> Payments received, which are not matched with invoices, have been inaccurately recorded.

The commas in the second version indicate that the system prevents any payments being matched with invoices; the first version merely refers to the (possibly few) payments not so matched. The first version limits, or defines, the kind of payments concerned; the second statement does not limit the class of payments, but adds another statement about the same subject; not only are they inaccurately recorded, but they are not matched with invoices. So much difference can a pair of commas make to the meaning.

commas joining independent clauses. See 'joining independent clauses'.

compare with – to. In nearly all business contexts, and in doubt, say 'compare with' something; not 'compare to':

> This makes a total of 10p per share *compared with* the previous year.
> The lower rate *compared with* the previous year arises from a change in the date of divided payment.

'Compare with' means to make a comparison with; 'compare to' means to be like, or more usually, 'not to be compared to' means to be unlike.

concrete and abstract. See p.34.

condition. See '-tion'. This word is long, abstract, and generally unnecessary, like 'case' and 'character'. It is a way of making a simple idea complicated:
Wrong: The accounts are in an unaudited condition.
Right: The accounts are unaudited.

consists of – in. 'Consists' can be followed by 'of' or 'in' depending on the meaning.

> Consits of = Is made of, is composed of
> Consists in = Is defined as; simply is

Stock *consists of* items available on call and obsolete items. Good marketing *consists in* maintaining a good public image.

contents or **table of contents.** This should be a list of chapters or sections and their page numbers near the beginning of a long report or a book. The sections are arranged in the Contents in the same order as they occur in the text. The Contents enables the reader to see the structure of the document, and to turn to the page of any section required. It is not to be confused with an index, which should be at the back of the document, and which arranges all the items, not only section headings, in alphabetical order. This book, like most non-fiction books, has both.

criteria. This is the plural of 'criterion', meaning a test or standard.
'The prospectus must meet both the legal requirements and the criteria imposed by the Stock Exchange.'

dash. The punctuation mark – is liable to lower the tone of a professional document, and is unnecessary. It can be used, and is, to replace any or all the other punctuation marks, and this makes it an imprecise means of communication to the reader. It is often used to introduce a list after a colon, but the colon can do that job adequately without help from the dash.

data. Plural. 'Data *are* not available at present.' The singular 'datum' does exist, but it is too rare to use without a definition.

different to – from. Pedants say that 'different to' must be wrong because we do not say 'differ to' but 'differ from'. The authorities deny the logic of this, and allow both 'different to' and 'different from'. However, there are so many pedants on this particular point to make 'different from' the only advisable version.

disinterested.
'We are not convinced that the advice of the firm collecting debts is disinterested.'
'A vested interest', we say, and 'an interested party', not meaning that they are curious but that they have something to gain.
'Disinterested' is the opposite of 'interested' in this sense only; do not confuse it with 'uninterested' meaning 'bored by'.

divided between – among. See 'between'.

doubt that – whether. If you doubt, you doubt whether; if you do not doubt, you do not doubt that.

due to. There is no need to use this slippery phrase when 'owing to' and 'because of' are available, and it would be wise to avoid. it. Strictly, it can only be an adjectival phrase; that is, it must have a specified noun in the sentence to refer to.
Right: The increase *due to* inflation has been ignored.
Wrong: We have not yet completed the report *due to* pressure of other work.
In the first sentence, 'due to' refers to the increase. In the second, there is nothing which is 'due to' except the delay, which is not mentioned. Neither 'we', nor 'the report', are due to pressure.

economic, economical. 'Economic' is a useful word, implying a serious financial calculation. 'Economical' is a long word for 'cheap' or 'unwasteful'.

e.g. from the Latin *exempli gratia* meaning 'for example'. See 'i.e.', with which it is so often confused that it is safer to stick to the English equivalents: 'for example', 'for instance', 'such as'.

either . . . or; neither . . . nor. The first principle is that it is wrong to follow 'either' with 'nor' unless there has been a previous negative such as 'not'; and it is always wrong to follow 'neither' with 'or'.

The second principle is that words which are outside the paired phrases, by coming before the first word of the pair, must apply to both phrases; and words inside one of the phrases cannot apply to the other:
Wrong: They *have* either forgotten or never knew.
Right: They either *have* forgotten or never knew.
Here 'have' does not apply to 'never knew', so 'have' should not be outside.
Wrong: They either *have* paid tax or been exempted.
Right: They *have* either paid tax or been exempted.
Here 'have' applies to 'been exempted' as well as to 'paid tax', and so should come outside both phrases.

The third principle is that 'neither' is the negative of 'either', and can sometimes be replaced by some other negative with 'either':
Right: 'Prices rose in neither the first nor the second half of the year.'
Right: 'Prices did not rise in either the first or the second half of the year.'

elegant variation. This is the practice of using different words for the same thing in a short passage, for fear of annoying the reader by repeating a word. Where a writer seems to be repeating a word by accident or negligence, it can offend, though writers are usually more sensitive about it than readers will be. The danger is that to avoid using the same word the writer will use another and the reader will wonder whether the meaning is different:

> All requests are entered on the company's internal order form so ensuring that no requisitions go astray.

The substitution of 'requests' and 'requisitions' for 'orders' could raise a doubt whether the internal order form is used for passing telephone messages as well as orders to buy. The repeated 'orders' and 'order' would do much less harm than the ambiguity of an elegant variation. Or use pronouns: '. . . that they do not go astray'.

enclosed please find. This common phrase suggests that the object is going to take some finding. Be brief: say 'we enclose'.

equal to.
Right: X is equal to Y.
Wrong: X is equal as Y.
Wrong: X is equal than Y.
Wrong: Turnover was equal if not greater than last year's.
Right: Turnover was equal to, if not greater than, last year's.

etc. Latin *etcetera* meaning 'and others'. This Latin tag is worth keeping, as it is not usually misplaced or ambiguous, and is shorter than the English equivalents. It can be overdone, and full English words like 'and so on' can look better than any abbreviation.

facilities. See '-ilities', of which this is the worst example. In the technical sense of borrowing arrangements it may be useful, but too often it is added when the writer has not thought whether it means anything and if so, what. See 'general', which can be compared with 'facilities' for vagueness of meaning. Sometimes it can be dropped without changing the meaning, as in 'transport facilities'.

factor. This word can often be omitted from phrases like 'the price factor' without changing the meaning; and as this is an abstract word, it should not pass unchallenged.

firstly. The authorities allow either 'first' or 'firstly' in the series, 'First I did this, secondly that, thirdly . . .'

Some pedants think that 'firstly' is wrong, or even that the word does not exist. It does, and can be used instead of 'first' in the series just mentioned. But as 'first' is shorter and offends nobody, it is preferable.

footnotes. If these are at the foot of the page they are distracting, not so much on the way down the page to read them, as on the way back to find the place and start again. If the footnote is a fact and not a reference to a source, put it in brackets in the text. If there are any references to source documents, put a number in the text and give the source in a section called 'References' at the end, which according to British Standard 4811 should come after the Recommendations and before the Appendices.

former, latter. Avoid this usage. It obliges the reader to look back to see what goes with what, an unnecessary distraction when you could have repeated the names of the things they stand for, or used pronouns.

general. Poor report writers often seem to need a heading to cover a few bits of information that do not fit elsewhere, and 'general' is one of the favourites for this purpose. It fails to meet the first requirement of a heading, which is to inform the reader roughly what is in the section underneath. If the section has no unity, rearrange the sections; if it has a unity, find a more revealing heading than 'General'. It might be justified if it was one of two sub-headings, the other being 'Particular', and the main heading told the rest of the story.

get or **got.** These are good words, but have been misused so often that they are now not welcome in many circles even when they are right. To play safe, find other words: have, acquire, possess etc.

global. See 'overall'. A global figure may be useful to distinguish one level of total from another, but it is more precise to refer to the area or period or activity to which the total refers.

glossary. Few technical reports have glossaries, but most of those which use technical terms would be better for them. Writers often do not know how well educated their readers are, and often they know that some of the readers are learned in the subject and some are beginners. So either specialist terms are not used, which insults the learned, or used but not defined, which is hard on the beginners, or defined when they first occur and used undefined later, which is a struggle for those who start at the back. The reader who reads the Conclusions first, by no means a rare or illogical person, may have to read the whole of the earlier part of the report just to find the definition needed to understand a few sentences at the end. The most efficient solution, for a report that ought to contain technical terms and will go to a wide range of readers, is to have a glossary of terms at the end, as the last appendix. This gives the beginners exactly what they want without disturbing the others.

hopefully.

'In a year we will hopefully have increased the overdraft.'

A few years ago this could only have meant that we would, by then, have increased the overdraft, full of the hope of using it and paying it back. Now it means that we are not certain, but only hope, to increase the overdraft. The word thus has come to mean 'let us hope', or 'with luck', a use which the *Oxford Paperback Dictionary* says many people regard as unacceptable. While the confusion lasts, it is advisable to avoid 'hopefully', saying 'we hope' or 'with luck' for one sense, and 'in hope' or 'with hope' or 'full of hope' for the other.

hyphens. The main rule is to leave out hyphens unless there is no other way of avoiding ambiguity. Clearly, a hyphen is the only way to distinguish a man eating fish from a man-eating fish. A story may be well read but only the reader can be well-read. Where an adverb precedes an adjective, an unnecessary hyphen often appears: well advised people do not write 'well-advised'.

I. See 'pronouns'.

i.e. Latin, *id est*, meaning 'that is'. It is frequently confused with 'e.g.', although its meaning is quite different; its meaning is closer to 'viz.' which is usually translated 'namely'. Even though English phrases are longer, they are safer to write because easier to understand: that is; which is; or; which means; in other words; the same things as.

if.

Credit notes were approved, if not initialled, by the Sales Manager.

This could mean: (1) The credit notes were approved, but not initialled, by . . .; or (2) The credit notes were at least approved, and possibly also initialled, by the Sales Manager; or (3) The Sales Manager only approved those notes which had not been previously initialled.

'If' implies that the approval depended on the lack of initialling, and so strictly the third meaning is the only correct one. For the first meaning, use 'but' or 'though' instead of 'if'; for meaning (2) some longer translation seems unavoidable; and even for (3) it would surely be advisable to reword the sentence to avoid misunderstanding.

-ilities. Avoid words ending -ility or -ilities; to some extent shun all words ending in -ity or -ities. They are long and abstract, and often rare and unnecessary. Once the habit of using these words takes hold, it can be hard to shake off. Shorter concrete expressions have greater practicability and utility, and possess more desirability and visualisability. In other words, they are more practicable and useful, desirable and pictorial.

in connection with, in regard to, in respect of, in terms of. These and other such phrases provide the processed cheese of professional writing: more adhesive than nourishing. Use them only when you cannot use the simpler equivalents: of, in, for, about, if, to, over, with etc.

index. See 'contents'.

infer – imply. These words are confused because they are connected, but different. Imply is a relationship between two: for example, in a report, the evidence implies the conclusions. Infer is a three-way relationship, in which a person infers one thing from another. The investigator infers the conclusions from the evidence. Conclusions are the *implications* of, or from, the facts; they are also *inferences* made by the investigator from the facts. A person can imply something, as well as inferring; for instance by making a statement which implies (hints at) something unsaid.

inst., ult., and **prox.** Avoid these Latin months; use the name of the month in English instead. Before these hoary old months slip from disrepute into oblivion, it is worth remembering A.P. Herbert's satirical love-lyric, published in 1935:

> I heard the happy lark exult
> Too soon, for it was early ult.,
> And now the land with rain is rinsed –
> Ah, mournful is the month of inst.;
> Love, like a lizard on the rocks,
> Is hungry for the suns of prox.
>
> Boy Cupid, with his catapult
> Could find but sorry sport in ult.;
> But through the woods, with bluebells chintzed,
> My lady comes to me in inst.:
> And O may Cupid speed the clocks,
> For she will marry me in prox.!

instance. See 'case'. The case against 'case' applies in this instance against 'instance'.

it. Do not begin a sentence with this word in its indefinite, impersonal sense. Phrases like 'It should be observed' or 'It seems appropriate to state at this point' can be omitted completely. Phrases that cannot be left out altogether can usually be shortened.

Wrong	*Right*
It is my understanding	I understand
It is manifest	Manifestly
It seems apparent	Apparently
It should be apparent	Apparently, Obviously
It will be noted	But note, Please note
It would be expedient to consider	Consider, Let us not overlook
It has been stated herein	I have already stated, As stated
It is interesting to note in this connection	Observe, Note however, But note
It should be added	Furthermore

jargon. This is an abusive word applied to other people's technical language. A reader who believes the writer is showing off, or trying to forestall criticism by writing so that no one can understand, works off irritation by saying 'Jargon!' Therefore, a writer who is not doing that, and is anxious to prove it, should define or explain terms (see 'glossary'); or else avoid using specialist language for non-specialist readers, which is likely to be more difficult.

joining independent clauses.
The fault. In our experience one of the most frequent serious grammatical mistakes people make is forming one sentence from independent clauses without a proper break between the clauses. We therefore discuss it at some length.

An independent clause is a group of words making sense by itself; it could stand as an independent sentence between full stops if necessary. In the first of the following sentences there are three, and in the other sentences two, independent main clauses; the 'joins' are inadequate throughout.

Wrong: The only real problem would appear to be the financing of short-term loans, these could be financed from government sources at the outset, however, there is a credit problem in the country.

Wrong: However, there was no apparent correlation to be found, a possible reason for this would be the sharing of commodities by two or more groups.

Wrong: It is almost impossible for local people on lower incomes to rent such property, it is these people who are in need of Council stock.

Wrong: Other aspects may affect our decision, we will postpone it until we receive your report.

Each of the commas above could be changed to a full stop; therefore the separate clauses are independent. Such clauses can only be joined if the punctuation is strengthened, or if a conjunction is added to the comma.

The punctuation remedy. The easiest remedy is to substitute a semicolon for the comma:

Right: The only real problem would appear to be the financing of short-term loans; these could be financed from government sources at the outset; however, there is a credit problem in the country.

If the sense and rhythm allow, a colon or full stop could replace the comma:

Right: The only real problem would appear to be the financing of short-term loans; these could be financed from government sources at the outset. However, there is a credit problem in the country.

If one of the clauses is a *dependent* clause, so that it does not make sense by itself and could not become a grammatical sentence, a comma is enough. Even a comma may be unnecessary.

Right: Other aspects may affect the decision, which we will postpone until we receive your report.

Right: Other aspects may affect the decision which we will postpone until we receive your report.

The conjunction remedy. You can join two or more independent clauses with a conjunction, with or without a comma:

Right: However, there was no apparent correlation to be found, *and* a possible reason for this would be the sharing of commodities by two or more groups.

Right: Other aspects may affect the decision *and* we will postpone it until we receive your report.

Now comes the problem. An adverb will not serve instead of a conjunction, and the distinction between adverbs and conjunctions is difficult. The authorities do not offer much help on this point, nor do the dictionaries, because many of the words that give difficulty are sometimes adverbs and sometimes conjunctions. The writer has to be able to test whether the particular word is an adverb or a conjunction in the particular context.

If the word joining the two independent clauses is a conjunction, it is not grammatically attached to either clause; it can therefore come in only one place, between the clauses. If it is an adverb, it belongs grammatically to the second clause, and there are usually two or more places in the second clause where it could go without changing the meaning.

To test whether the word joining two clauses is an adverb or a conjunction, try putting the word to be tested somewhere after the first word in the second clause. Mark the word off with commas if necessary. If the sentence makes sense and means the same as before, with possibly a shift of emphasis, it is an adverb. If moving the tested word gives a different or absurd result, the word is a conjunction.

Let us see if 'therefore' is an adverb or conjunction in one of our sentences:

1. Other aspects may affect our decision; *therefore* we will postpone it until we receive your report.
2. Other aspects may affect our decision; we will *therefore* postpone it until we receive your report.
3. Other aspects may affect our decision; we will postpone it, *therefore*, until we receive your report.

'Therefore' is clearly movable within the second clause without changing the meaning. If you try the same test with 'and' or 'so', they make sense in the position occupied by 'therefore' in sentence 1, but nowhere else. It follows that 'therefore' is an adverb, but 'and' and 'so' are here conjunctions. The break in the sentence cannot be made by a comma with 'therefore'. In front of 'therefore' there must be either a semicolon, to make a break between the clauses, or a conjunction such as 'and' or 'so'. These conjunctions can make a break without a semicolon, and even without punctuation mark at all.

It may help to remember one reason for this rule. Movable adverbs often come at the end of clauses they belong to. If you put a movable adverb between two clauses, it could belong to either, and would be ambiguous, unless a clear division showed where one clause ended and the next began. In the next sentence, the movable 'however' could belong to the first or the second clause, and one or other of the commas should be a semicolon to explain to the reader how to understand it.

> The only real problem would appear to be the financing of short-term loans. These could be financed from government sources at the outset, *however*, there is a credit problem in the country.

The following lists indicate some of the words useful in joining clauses, and show whether for this purpose they are likely to be adverbs or conjunctions:

Adverbs: also, however, indeed, meanwhile, moreover, nevertheless, otherwise, perhaps, therefore, well.

Conjunctions: although, and, because, but, for, if, nor, or, so, unless, until, while.

Latin abbreviations. Latin presents problems, and so do abbreviations; Latin abbreviations are doubly objectionable. Some have worked themselves into common usage and are not easily replaced, for example, etc., A.D., N.B., P.S., a.m. and p.m. Avoid others if you can. In this appendix, see e.g., i.e., inst., and viz.

lower, smaller, fewer, and **less.** 'Lower' and 'smaller' are easy to handle and can be followed by a singular or plural:

'Lower prices' or 'a smaller price'.

'Fewer' means 'a smaller number of':

'Fewer sales', but not 'Fewer profits'.

'Less' means 'a smaller amount of'; it must be followed by a singular:

'Less expense', but not 'Less expenses'.

It is not idiomatic to put 'a' in front of 'less': 'That is of less value', but not 'A less value would be appropriate'; it has to be 'A lower value', or similar.

majority. 'The majority of' is a long-winded version of 'most'.

mind. 'With this in mind' is often long-winded for 'so'.

nature. See 'character'. Clauses of an abstract and long-winded nature are also clauses of an unnecessary character; or, the abstract noun 'nature' is unnecessary.

none.
None of the claims are outstanding.
None of the claims is outstanding.
There are no outstanding claims.
The authorities allow all three versions. However, pedants object to the first on the grounds that 'none' means 'not one' and should be followed by a singular verb; and the second looks wrong at first reading because the singular 'is' comes so soon after the plural 'claims'. The only way to keep out of trouble is to use the third version or some similar rewording.

numbering. It seems pointless, and even dangerous, to number pages, paragraphs, chapters, appendices, or anything else, if there is only one of them. The reasons for having a number do not apply and the reader may waste time looking for number 2.

numbers: words or numerals? Prefer words (one, two, three) to numerals (1, 2, 3) at the beginning of a sentence, and for numbers up to ten. Prefer numerals to words for numbering (for example of pages, paragraphs, etc.) and for numbers over ten.

For two numbers in succession, it is clearer if one is a word and one a numeral: 'Fifteen £40 instalments'.

of course. Avoid this phrase. It means literally 'you do not need me to tell you'; and if that is true the whole sentence is unnecessary. Modified, it means 'please excuse me for mentioning something so obvious', which wil offend the reader who does not think it obvious at all. In journalism it may be used to impress, to show familiarity with some obscure fact: 'Lady Betty Bootle is, *of course*, the sister-in-law of the Duchess of Peebles.' In professional writing there is a risk that the reader will interpret 'of course' as a piece of showing off. Often the piece of information in the 'of course' clause can be inserted without either telling the readers you know they know already, or appearing to assume that they have not

heard of it. One way is to put the 'of course' part in a subordinate clause beginning 'as':
Wrong: The accounting policy on the valuation of leasehold premises will, *of course*, be changing at the end of this financial year. We are writing to let you know the additional information required.
Right: As the accounting policy on the valuation of leasehold premises is changing at the end of this financial year, we are writing to let you know the additional information required.

one (pronoun). Avoid 'one' as a pronoun. Once one has started one's writing using 'one' one finds it difficult to regain one's freedom; and it becomes tedious.

only.
'Letters containing professional advice should only be signed by a partner.' The practical meaning of this is perhaps clear enough, but strictly it means that someone else should write the letter; the partner should have nothing to do with it except to put a signature at the bottom. 'Only' is both an adjective and an adverb, and can qualify many of the words in a long sentence. When it changes its place in the sentence it changes the meaning of the sentence, and in some places it will leave the meaning ambiguous. Here, if the meaning is that no one except a partner should sign such letters, the 'only' should come after 'by':

> 'Letters including professional advice should be signed by only a partner'.

However, this is not an idiomatic or happy version. Sometimes the sentence is clear without an 'only'; sometimes the sentence needs to be rewritten: 'Letters including professional advice should not be signed except by a partner.'

overall. This word (not 'over-all') is useful for measured quantities between extremes, as in 'overall length', or to distinguish between different kinds of total, though surely 'sub-total', 'total', and 'grand-total' ought to be enough. A more precise adjective would be better: 'National total'. In 'overall review' or 'overall responsibility' or describing some other unmeasurable thing, again a precise noun or adjective is better: 'Company review', or 'divisional responsibility'.

per. This was a Latin word, and even the authorities are reluctant to admit that it is now English. In 'miles per hour', 'earnings per share', 'sales per employee', and many other ratios, it has become essential. Use it freely with English units except perhaps 'per year', for which many still prefer 'per annum'. 'Per second', 'per month', and so on should give no trouble.

percentage. Avoid using 'a percentage of' as a means of lending spurious scientific accuracy to a statement meaning only 'some' or 'a number of', as in 'A percentage of the employees have not considered ways of improving productivity.'

phenomena; phenomenal; phenomenon. These mean merely 'events', 'apparent', and 'event' respectively, for which they are long-winded translations. The meaning 'extraordinary' is best kept for speech.

position. See '-tion' and 'situation'. Avoid phrases like 'the liquidity position' when 'liquidity' by itself is enough; and avoid phrases like 'we will maintain our position', when the meaning is not precise; and phrases like 'we are not yet in a position', which suggests that you have temporarily lost your balance.

Practical – practicable. These words are often confused. Avoid them, except when using 'practical' to contrast with 'theoretical'. 'Practical' means useful, 'practicable' means workable. The opposites are unpractical and impracticable. A plan which is successfully carried out must be practicable, but may be unpractical. 'Practicable' is a mouthful, which no doubt explains why people often say 'a practical proposition' when they mean 'practicable'; and equivalents like 'feasible' and 'possible' are little better. The best substitute may be a phrase like 'can be achieved'. 'Practically' is a special danger because the two meanings, 'nearly' and 'in practice', are conflicting.

preposition at the end of a sentence. A preposition is a short word like 'in', 'to', or 'by', that normally precedes a noun; and pedants say that it should do so always, and hence that ending a sentence with a preposition is wrong. The authorities call this a superstition. Sometimes a preposition at the end is clumsy:

> The balance sheet should show the estimated amount of any capital expenditure which has been authorised by the Board of Directors but which contracts have not been placed for.

Better: . . . but for which contracts have not been placed.

On the other hand, take Gowers's example where the preposition at the end is clearer, 'What did you choose that book to be read to out of for', which ends with four prepositions. It would be pompous to say 'For what did you choose that book out of which I am to read to you?'

presently. Avoid this word because it means 'now' to some people and 'soon' to others. There are many unambiguous substitutes for both meanings.

prima facie. Latin; prefer English translations like 'at first sight', 'on the first impression', 'superficially', or 'at first glance'.

prior to. Prefer 'before'.

pronouns. Passages are easier to read for the 'you', 'they', 'we', 'I', 'my', 'our', and the rest. A personal tone is more acceptable to most people than the impersonal, at least to this extent. Frequent 'I' is irritating and does sound self-important, but 'we' does not have that defect and can lend authority to a passage.

proportion. This is a good word if used precisely of the measured relation between two measurable units, but it is debased when it means vaguely 'some'; see 'percentage'.

proposition. Avoid this. 'Proposal' or 'idea' may serve if a noun is essential, but often 'proposition' adds nothing, as in 'Complete retooling is not an economic proposition' which means 'Complete retooling is not economic'.

purchase. Prefer the short, ordinary, Saxon 'buy'.

quantify. Before using this word, check that the more ordinary and shorter words 'measure' or 'assess' will not serve better.

quite.
The reserves have been quite exhausted.
The news was quite good.
In the first sentence 'quite' means 'completely'; in the second it means 'fairly'. Ensure the context makes the meaning clear, or else find another word.

quotation marks and punctuation. If the punctuation mark applies to the quotation, so that in effect the punctuation mark is also quoted, it should go inside the quotation marks. If it applies to the surrounding sentence, it should go outside the quotation marks. The question mark is correctly inside in 'What is its break-up value?' But if there should be two punctuation marks, as when both quotation and the sentence round it end together, do not put two punctuation marks. Choose one; the following guidelines, and sentences to illustrate, may help:

1. A comma outside the quotation overrides a full stop inside:
   I said 'I want to see the books', but nobody listened.
2. A question mark inside a quotation overrides a comma outside:
   I said 'Isn't three months' rent owing?' but nobody took any notice.
3. A question mark outside the quotation overrides a full stop inside:
   Why did she say 'You owe three months' rent'?
4. A question mark outside the quotation overrides a question mark inside:
   Why did she say 'Isn't three months' rent owing'?

re. Lawyers may need this Latin word, but no one else does. Estate agents sometimes head their letters 'Re Wistaria Lodge, Kitchener Rd' but the 're' is always useless in a heading. It can be an all-purpose preposition, as in 'We return your cheque on a/c re commission re Mr Pim's agreement re Slingby's Soups'. It is easier for the reader if the correct preposition is used, bringing the writing into sharper focus: 'on', 'for', 'about', or whatever is closest to the meaning.

regard. 'In regard to', 'as regards', 'with regard to'. Simple short substitutes are 'in', 'for', 'with', 'about', 'on', etc. and are preferable. They are more effective. Keep 'regard' as a verb meaning 'see' or 'look at', and as a noun, meaning 'admiration'.

relation. 'In relation to', is a long-winded phrase for 'over' or one of the other prepositions given with 'regard'.

remember. 'You will remember' suffers from the same paradox as 'of course'; either it is untrue, or the words that follow are unnecessary. Often it means, if you ever knew, you have forgotten'. As with 'of course' the answer may be a subordinate clause:
Wrong: You will remember we agreed to use metric measurements, and I have amended the letter accordingly.
Right: I have amended the letter to conform to our agreement to use metric measurements.

repetition. See 'elegant variation'.

report on. There seems to be no reason for the title of a report to be, for instance, 'Report on Word-Processing Equipment' rather than just 'Word-Processing Equipment'. The only justification would be if the report were liable to be confused with another kind of document, such as a list of parts, on the same subject. Headings should be short, and it should be obvious that a report is a report. We do not head letters 'Letter on Invoice No. 1973'.

respect. 'with respect'; 'with respect to'. In committee someone may say 'with respect, I suggest . . .' meaning 'I respect you personally but I disagree with you about this'. The effect is much like saying 'I am about to attack you'. Avoid writing the phrase. 'With respect to' is a long-winded prepositional phrase; see 'regard' and 'relation', with which it is comparable.

same, the same. Use ordinary pronouns, such as 'it', 'them', or 'this', instead of 'same' or 'the same' in sentences like this:
Wrong: We enclose invoices and I will be pleased if you will check and return same.

service, to. The noun 'service' is vague and ambiguous; as a verb, 'to service' is both vague and inelegant. In the sense of paying interest, as in 'to service this loan' it should be defined or avoided.

shall and **will, should** and **would.** If you do not understand by instinct which word is correct in a particular sentence, submit your writing to a colleague who does understand. The full scholarly explanation in *The King's English* covers 20 pages; it is not easy reading, but anything shorter would be an over-simplification.

situation.
'a bad debt situation'
'the security situation'
'we could not avoid this situation'.
The word has been fashionable for a long time, for use when it is unnecessary and to replace a precise word; and it is now better to avoid it even when it is needed for its original meaning, 'place'.

split infinitive. An infinitive is made up of two words. The first word is 'to' and the second is the verb. Examples are 'to ensure' or 'to develop'. (In the past infinitive that seems to have more than two words, 'to have ensured', strictly the infinitive is only 'to have'.) Splitting the infinitive means putting a word, usually an adverb, between these two words: '*to* definitely *ensure*', '*to* carefully *develop*'. Pedants condemn split infinitives completely. The authorities do not.

If the adverb is not to go between 'to' and the verb, it has to go somewhere else in the sentence, and there is a risk of ambiguity. 'The Board discussed the proposal carefully to develop the site' might mean that the discussion was careful; and indeed the reader might take that to be the meaning, with 'carefully' placed anywhere except inside the infinitive. It must always be better to split an infinitive than to run the risk of misleading your reader. It may take time to find an unambiguous version without a split infinitive, such as 'The Board considered the proposal for a careful development of the site'. For an important document, or for critical readers, it is worth searching for a version that does not upset the pedants and is not ambiguous. If the search is unjustifiably difficult, the split infinitive is better than the ambiguity.

subject–verb agreement. Singular subjects require singular verbs: plural subjects plural verbs. The noun closest to the verb is not necessarily the subject:
Wrong: A *group* of firms *were* involved.
Right: A *group* of firms *was* involved.
The following words all take a singular verb: Anybody, anyone, each, every, everybody, everyone, kind, and sort (but 'kinds' and 'sorts' take plural verbs). See 'none' and 'either'.

Two or more subjects joined by 'and' become plural: 'The *establishment* and *maintenance* of an adequate system of internal control *are* the responsibility of the directors'.

When several subjects are joined by 'or', the verb can agree with the nearest subject, which again is not necessarily the nearest noun: 'The partners, or the principal partner concerned, or the *audit manager* monitoring the subsidiary companies, *is* entitled to call a meeting'. But if this principle yields a sentence that looks or feels wrong, find some way of recasting it so that the reader is not troubled by the grammatical problem.

subjunctives. The authorities say that the subjunctive is dying; but there is still some life in the subjunctive verb 'to be'.
Present: I be, you be, he, she, or it be, we be, they be;
Past: I were, you were, he, she or it were, we were, they were.
This is used in formal resolutions:

I move the auditors be reappointed.

It is used in 'if . . . were' clauses expressing an idea not a fact:

If it *were* thought necessary to continue this control . . . (implying it is not thought necessary).

If the information required to be given in a prospectus *were* not specified . . . (implying it is specified).

But: We asked *if* it *was* true that the correspondence had been destroyed . . . (implying that the facts are not known).

target. In business and management this word has an indispensable meaning: a planned amount, a budget objective, a maximum cost or minimum output to be achieved. We have short-term, simple, compromise, or limited targets; we have to set, review, and achieve targets; above all, we measure performance against target. To Sir Ernest Gowers, who presumably had no need to use the word outside archery, it was natural to ridicule those who appeared to be stretching the metaphor by fighting for targets, or being a long way behind them. Today this use of 'target' is no longer a metaphor stretched; it is a good new meaning for a good old word.

terms. 'in terms of'. Use a simple preposition if possible, or omit the phrase completely.
Wrong: In terms of profits the year was a record.
Right: It was a record year *for* profits.

through. The American expression 'Friday through Monday' means what in British English is called 'Friday to Monday inclusive'. If there is some doubt about the exact time meant, it is safer to use the phrase with 'inclusive', as the other version, though shorter, is not always understood. If the doubt is not important or does not exist, 'Friday to Monday' is enough.

-tion. Words ending in -tion or -tions are abstract nouns, sometimes necessary, often not. Avoid them, particularly if they are long, vague, and ambiguous, as they often are. See 'condition', 'position', and 'situation'. Habitual use of -tion words leads to this sort of aesthetic ugliness and intellectual vagueness:

The cessation of the exemptions on information should be based on the observations of the Board of Trade, a consideration of public security, and representations from financial institutions.

transportation. One meaning of this word is the banishment of a criminal to a penal settlement. See '-tion'. Do not use it instead of 'transport'; if you have a technical reason for needing both words, define them so that the difference is clear to the readers.

unattached participles. 'Climbing the hill, the sea is just visible.' As the sea was not climbing anything, 'climbing' is an unattached participle. Participles are verbal adjectives: a *covering* letter, *misinformed* people, the individual *returning* correspondence. They are verbal because they come from the verbs 'cover', 'misinform', and 'return'. They are adjectives describing 'letter', 'people', and 'individual' respectively. Adjectives require nouns that they describe. An unattached participle is a verbal adjective with no noun stated:

Covering the year ended 31st March 1980, it would be advisable to meet the buyer's representatives.
Misinformed about the valuation, the documents were incomplete.
Before returning the signed accounts to us for signature as auditors, the following points should be dealt with.

In these examples the words 'covering', 'misinformed', and 'returning' do not describe any noun in the sentence. Therefore the writer must either change the participle:

To cover the year ended . . .

or supply a noun to which the participle can be logically attached:

We were *misinformed* about the valuation and . . .
Before *returning* the signed accounts to us for signature as auditors, *you* need to deal with the following points.

Those who find this advice difficult to apply, should take the precaution of avoiding participles, and in particular avoid a word ending '-ing', near the beginning of a sentence.

under the circumstances. The authorities allow this phrase, as well as '*in* the circumstances'; pedants object to 'under'. Prefer the shorter, as well as the safer, version: 'in the circumstances'.

very. This word has, we think, been worked to death. 'Very Urgent' has no more force than 'Urgent', except in organisations that take the trouble to give both words a specific meaning. To put 'Very Confidential' on a document would be absurd. To strengthen an adjective, find a more descriptive adverb than 'very', which may well only weaken it.

viable. Avoid this word. It is in vogue as a substitute for 'economic', 'profitable', 'good', 'capable of making profits', 'capable of growth', and 'worth discussing'. The more popular it becomes the less precise its meaning.

view. 'In our view' may be a suitable substitute for 'we believe'. Most of the other 'view' phrases are unnecessary: 'In view of' could be 'because of' or 'as'; 'From the point of view of' could be 'to' or 'for' or something similar; 'To express a view about' means 'to comment'; and 'With a view to' is simply 'to' or 'for'.

viz. This is a Latin abbreviation meaning 'namely', which is a better word to use. See 'i.e.'.

with a view to. See 'view'.

with regard to. See 'regard'.

Index